The Official Taxpayer's Guide to Solving Your IRS Tax Problems

Larry M. Weinstein, CPA
Certified Tax Resolution Specialist

Director of National Tax Practice
www.SolveMyTaxProblems.com

9639 Hillcroft, Suite 820
Houston, Texas 77096
(713) 726-1603 voice
(832) 202-2500 fax

Larry@SolveMyTaxProblems.com

This book presents information that is factual as of the time of publication. The information presented here is of a general nature. How the IRS rules and regulations should best be applied is different in every taxpayer's unique case. Accordingly, no liability can be assumed in how the information is applied to your particular personal situation.

No client relationship has been created or can be inferred by purchase of this book.

Table of Contents

Introduction

An IRS Tax Problem is something that anyone may have to face. I should know. As a CPA and Certified Tax Resolution Specialist for the past 18 years, I have worked with hundreds of clients to resolve their IRS Tax Problems.

The vast majority of my clients are honest, hard-working people. They certainly did not just wake up one morning and decide that they weren't going to pay the IRS.

The common thread, in my experiences as a tax specialist, seems to be an unfortunate turn of events in a person's life which challenges that person's ability to pay the IRS. It may be the loss of employment, a failed business venture, a divorce, or perhaps the death of a loved one. Some of my clients have battled serious illnesses, or suffer from alcoholism, or drug addiction.

These are problems that any one of us may have to face, and one of the unfortunate end results is that paying taxes may become virtually impossible.

If you find yourself with an IRS Tax Problem, before you have to take any action, there are some things you should know.

First, you are not alone. Approximately 20 million other taxpayers are facing an IRS Tax Problem at any one time.

Second, you need to know that there ***is*** a solution to your problem.

The IRS Collection Division has numerous programs to help taxpayers get back into the tax system and to help them put together plans to resolve their tax debts.

One of them can and will work for you!

Third, you must take action as soon as possible to begin to solve your problem.

Once you realize that you are not alone, that there is a solution and that it's up to you to take action to address it, you're well on the way to putting your tax problems behind you.

This book will help you decide on the correct course of action and point you in the right direction to resolve your tax issues in the way that's most favorable for you, and not just for the IRS.

What to do if you have an IRS Problem?

If you find yourself with an IRS Tax Problem, the single most important thing you can do is this: do not ignore it.

Once the IRS Collection Division has you in their sights, they won't stop their pursuit until there is a resolution. The problem simply won't go away by itself.

Over time the problem will only get bigger and more expensive. If you don't file your taxes, the IRS will do it for you. And the taxes due will likely be higher than if you filed them yourself.

If you have a balance due, penalties and interest continue to accrue, sometimes equaling the original amount of tax owed.

It is up to you to gather as much information as possible and to begin to deal with the problem. It may be that you do not owe as much as the IRS says that you do. *It may be that you owe nothing at all.* And in some instances, you may even be due a refund. But you must act quickly, because you don't have forever to claim your refund.

If you need more help than you find in this book, please note that I accept a limited number of new clients each month. You can call and check on availability in my schedule – but it's most likely that you will find the help you need in the pages that follow.

Why I wrote this book

I'm a CPA. Every day I work with taxpayers who have all sorts of IRS Tax Problems.

Usually my clients come to me feeling frustration, despair, or fear. They are hard-working, honest people, most of whom have never had any problems with the IRS in their entire lives. They've always filed their taxes. They've always paid their taxes. And now the IRS says that they owe money.

Make no mistake about it. The IRS is relentless in collecting taxes they think are due them.

The big question I used to always ask myself is "*Why?*"

Why do taxpayers worry needlessly for years?...when they may not owe any money at all?...when they may owe much less than the IRS says that they do?...and when there are solutions to their problems?

People should know that there are ways to relieve their IRS headaches, get the IRS out of their lives, and get their lives back on track. There are ways to eliminate the stress that their problems put on their finances and their personal lives.

I have seen families' personal lives torn apart by IRS problems. I am aware of families who have suffered almost unbearably, and the real tragedy is that help was available, and they didn't get to it soon enough.

It troubles me greatly. But I have come to the conclusion that people simply don't understand that dealing with the fear of the unknown (what it would be like dealing with the IRS) is *actually much less painful* than the fear of the known (what it feels like doing nothing to deal with their IRS problems).

What I've also found in case after case is that even though my clients could have saved themselves much time, aggravation and money just by coming in to see me, they didn't have enough information to understand exactly what their problem was.

And once they understood what the problem was, they didn't have a handle on all of the options that were available to help solve their problems.

So, I wrote this book. I wrote it for you. I wrote it to help you clearly understand exactly what your IRS problem is, and the many solutions available to help you solve your problem.

I trust that you will find it easy to read and understand, and that it will answer your questions.

If after reading this book you find that you still have questions, or think that you might need professional help in dealing with the IRS, give me a call at the office.

I remain dedicated to solving your IRS Tax Problems.

Larry M. Weinstein, CPA
Certified Tax Resolution Specialist
Houston, Texas

Common IRS Myths

1) If you ignore the problem, it will go away by itself.

The operations section of the IRS Collection Division is designed after that of a finance company or bill collection agency.

They are designed to do one thing and one thing only: Collect taxes that they think are due to them. Once they have you in their computers as owing them money, it is *up to you* to either prove that you don't owe them money, or perhaps that you owe a different, lesser amount. But *you must take the initiative*.

The IRS makes extensive use of computers to keep track of what they think taxpayers owe them. They send out a series of increasingly threatening letters, asking for payment of the tax due.

Their only obligation is to send the correspondence to the last known address of record. While some taxpayers think that they are hiding from the IRS by moving and not sending notice of a forwarding address, this is simply ineffective.

The IRS is required only to try and make contact with you. If they don't have a good address for you, or you fail to sign for a registered letter, the fact that they made the attempt to contact you is all that the IRS must prove.

Therefore, it may be a wise idea to complete a Form 8822-Change of Address or otherwise update the IRS as to your correct address. This may help prevent nasty "enforced collection" surprises.

2) What the IRS says that you owe is correct. Go ahead and pay it. They never make mistakes.

Feel free to go ahead and do this if money is not a problem for you. But please note that you may be making a mistake: often, the amount the IRS says that you owe is wrong.

This can be due to several factors.

First, the IRS may not have given you credit for all of the tax payments you've actually made. Or if they did give you credit, they may have given you credit for the wrong time periods, causing interest and penalties to be overstated.

Second, if the IRS has filed a return on your behalf (technically known as a Substitute for Return), the amount of tax due can be overstated if you have 1099-MISC Income from self-employment income.

The IRS will simply take the summation of the 1099s reported to them, add them up, and call them net self-employment income. They are permitted to do this, and that's what will happen, even if you had expenses like employees, rent, cost of sales, utilities, etc. The IRS makes no attempt to estimate the expenses that you may have incurred, only the income.

Third, the IRS may have adjusted a tax return that you have filed because you mistakenly omitted items of Stock Transactions, which should be reported on a 1099-B. The IRS does a similar thing here as they do with self-employment income, noted above.

If you fail to report capital gains transactions, the IRS will amend your return by simply including the net proceeds and net gain on your tax return.

No attempt is made to determine what the cost basis is. However, to provide an *accurate* picture of what you actually owe, the cost basis (what you paid for the stock) should be subtracted out of the sales proceeds to determine the true net gain or loss on the sale of the stock. Failure to do so will result in an overstatement of your income from capital gains, and it will overstate your taxes as well.

The only way to pay the *correct* amount of tax is simply to file a complete and accurate tax return.

If the IRS prepares your return for you or amends your return, rest assured that it will generally require you to pay more taxes than if you had prepared them correctly in the first place.

3) The IRS wants to settle your debt for the correct amount.

Once the IRS makes an assessment (see #2 above), they begin collection activity. The Collection Division does not care if the amount they are trying to collect is correct, or whether it is over- or understated.

If there is a balance recorded on their books, IRS Collections will try and collect it – even though it is through their own efforts that the tax may be overstated on the Substitute for Return or IRS Amended Return that the IRS may have filed for you.

If you think – or know – the balance is incorrect, it is up to you to work within the system, and correct the amount.

4) The US Income Tax system is illegal and I'm not even required to pay taxes.

Many erroneous arguments have been made by tax protestors over the years. None of them are valid.

If you don't think that income tax is legal, let me invite you to go to Tax Court and sit in front of a judge who pays his taxes and a jury who pay their taxes, and tell me what the outcome is!!

5) The IRS doesn't have the right to garnish my paycheck.

The IRS *does* have the right to do so and *will* garnish your wages. Depending upon how much you earn, they can take as much as 76% of your wages. The amount left in your paycheck may not be enough to cover your monthly living expenses.

You have until the next payday from the date your employer receives a wage garnishment notice, before your employer must begin withholding money from your paycheck. You must work quickly to keep the IRS from taking your paycheck.

The other problem that a wage garnishment causes is that your employer will now find out about your tax problems. Not only will your employer (and perhaps others at your place of employment) find out that you have an IRS Tax Problem – they will also find out how much you owe the IRS and for exactly what years you owe them.

This may not be seen in a positive light by your employer.

6) The IRS can't take money out of my bank account.

The IRS does have the right and will seize/levy your bank account. A bank levy "freezes" the money in your account, on the day the bank receives the notice of levy.

You then have 21 days from the date your bank receives the notice of levy to resolve your problem with the IRS and keep the IRS from taking the money in your bank account.

A bank levy/seizure causes all outstanding checks that you have at the time of the levy to be dishonored, or "bounce."

This may result in Non-Sufficient Funds charges from both your bank and the payee of any outstanding checks, also potentially harming your credit rating.

7) The IRS can't take my house.

Unfortunately, this is another myth that has been perpetuated over time. While it is true that it is harder for the IRS to seize your house than to garnish your wages or freeze your bank account, it can be and is still being done on a regular basis.

Most often though, this is done in the most extreme of circumstances, if all other types of enforced collections including liens and bank and wage levies have failed to get the taxpayer to deal with the problem.

The IRS must have a judge sign off on their plans to seize a house, so this action is reserved for the most serious of problems.

8) The IRS is interested in finding the best solution to my problem.

Unfortunately, that is not true. The IRS is interested in settling your case as quickly as possible. They are only interested in getting the maximum amount of money from you, the taxpayer, in the shortest amount of time, and at the least possible collection cost for the IRS.

Whether a particular solution to an IRS Tax Problem is the most appropriate for the taxpayer is of little concern to the IRS.

9) Can't I just settle my debts for "Pennies on the Dollar?"

Unfortunately, many of the companies which have sprung up offering IRS "Pennies on the Dollar" settlements are preying on fear and the lack of education of taxpayers with IRS problems. See the Bonus Chapter, The Truth Behind The "Pennies on the Dollar" Tax Representation Firms Finally Revealed.

What causes taxpayers to have IRS problems?

Not filing a tax return
If you don't file your tax return, the IRS may eventually prepare one on your behalf. They will generally only prepare a return when it would show a balance due. They do this in order to "make an assessment" so that they can begin Enforced Collection Activities.

However, if it is determined by the IRS that you are due a refund, they will not go to the trouble of preparing and filing a return for you. Technically, you're not in trouble with the IRS if you haven't filed a tax return, as long as you don't owe them any money. However, it is probably to your advantage to file properly, because if you're due a refund, you'll never get it unless you file.

Having a balance due
Sometimes taxpayers file their tax returns and there is a balance due to the IRS. This could be caused by withdrawal of pension proceeds, stock transactions, or other financial income such as interest or dividends for which no tax was taken out or no estimated tax payments were made, or if estimated tax payments were made which were simply too small.

Another possible reason for a balance due is that the IRS prepared your return for you – as noted above.

Adjustment of tax return by IRS

Some taxpayers have their originally filed returns amended by the IRS. The IRS typically will not change your return to decrease your tax or increase your refund. Some of the reasons that the IRS might adjust a tax return would include: having a problem with a dependent's Social Security Number; understatement of income (W-2s were omitted or 1099s were omitted if you file a Schedule C - Profit or Loss from Business [Sole Proprietorship]); or the IRS questions itemized deductions such as charitable contributions or business expenses if you filed a Schedule C.

In all instances, the IRS will ask you for proof or substantiation of expenses, or a reason why income they say you haven't reported, shouldn't be reported, according to you.

If you don't respond to IRS requests for information or clarification, the IRS will eventually adjust your tax return to the amounts that they feel are correct.

Failure to respond to IRS notices

In all instances, the IRS will not arbitrarily change your account to what they feel the balance should be.

If you haven't filed your return, they will ask you many times to file one before they file one for you.

If they think you owe them money, they will ask you many times for payment, before they start Enforced Collection Activity.

If they think your return is incorrectly stated, they will ask you for additional substantiation, before they adjust your account.

If you fail to provide any supporting documentation or substantiation or if your response is deemed to be inadequate, an adjustment, generally in favor of the IRS, will be made.

The IRS will be in what seems like constant contact with you, sending you these notices as well as their requests for information, through the mail.

Therefore, it is important to open any letters you receive from the IRS and see what is involved.

In many instances, if the trouble is dealt with early, the problem will less difficult to solve than if the problem is left alone.

What are some of the Enforced Collections Activities the IRS can use?

Levy

A levy is an enforced collection action taken by the IRS which seizes assets or income owned by a taxpayer.

Levies can be placed on:

- bank accounts
- savings accounts
- retirement accounts
- wages (garnishment)
- accounts receivables (for a business)

Bank Levies

If the IRS levies your bank account, they do so by sending a notice of levy to your bank. The day the bank receives the levy, it "freezes" your bank account for the lesser of the amount of the levy, or the entire balance of your account.

For example, the IRS issues a bank levy in the amount of $1,000. If you have $5,000 in your account on the day that the levy is received by the bank, the bank will "freeze" $1,000 of your money, leaving the remaining $4,000 in your account alone. If your account has $200 on the day that the bank receives the levy, you entire balance will be “frozen,” since it is less than the levy amount.

The funds that are frozen remain in your account, but are unavailable for twenty-one days. You have this time period to work with the IRS and get the levy released.

If you do not take action within 21 days, your bank will send the money that was “frozen” to the IRS. These funds will be applied against your tax debt to pay it in full, or reduce the amount owed.

To get the levy released, you must work with the IRS to find an alternate solution to pay your debt. These may include: filing an Installment Agreement; having your account placed in Currently-not-Collectible status; or filing an Offer in Compromise, all of which I will explain shortly.

The levy affects only the balance in your account on the date of the levy.

A bank levy is only good for the date on which it was originally issued. This means that you should always deposit additional funds immediately to cover outstanding checks. You may do so (and should do so) without fear that the IRS will take those funds as well.

This will keep you from receiving NSF check charges from your bank. It will also keep the payees of the outstanding checks from charging you additional fees, and it will help preserve your credit standing with them.

If your tax liability with the IRS is still not cleared after this levy, the IRS must start over and issue a new bank levy to obtain additional funds from your bank account.

Wage Levies

If the IRS levies your wages, the levy is sent to your employer. Your employer will be required to pay a large portion of your paycheck to the IRS until your tax debt is settled.

Your employer is required by law to honor the IRS levy, beginning with your next scheduled paycheck.

The IRS does not take all of your paycheck. They allow you to be paid the standard deduction amount plus the personal exemption amount based upon your filing status and number of dependents.

For example, if your filing status is single with one dependent (yourself), you would be allowed to keep $8,450 for the year. This equates to $162.50 per week or $704.16 per month. The amount that you earn above and beyond these amounts must be paid by your employer to the IRS.

The levy on your wages will only end if:

- The levy is released by the IRS;
- Your tax debts are paid off; or
- The statute of limitation prevents the collection of the taxes. I will discuss this in detail later.

IRS bank and wage levies are some of the most onerous and intrusive actions that the IRS can take in the collection process. They are the most disruptive to your life or business, and quick action is called for to get such levies released.

Federal Tax Lien

A tax lien is the Federal government's statutory right to your property for the amount of tax owed.

"Property" consists of any or all of your assets including your land, your home, any vehicles you own, as well as promissory notes, or any accounts receivable. The lien affects ALL current property as well as any property you may acquire AFTER the lien.

For the lien to be valid, the IRS must send you a Notice of Tax Due and Demand for Payment. You are given ten days from the date of the notice to pay your debt. If you have not paid your debt within this ten-day period, the lien on your property arises by law.

After that time, the lien exists automatically whether you are notified or not. This lien is imposed retroactively back to the date of the tax assessment. The IRS needs to take no further action for the lien to be valid.

Liens differ from levies in one very distinct way. The lien is a **right** to your property; the levy is a **seizure** of that property.

In the language of Letter 1058, the IRS "may file a Notice of Federal Tax Lien at any time to protect the government's interest." Remember, this lien already exists under law. In order for the IRS to protect its interest however, the lien must be "perfected."

Perfecting a lien simply means that the IRS must file a Notice of Federal Tax Lien (NFTL). This action formally stakes out the IRS' claim on your property.

The Letter 1058 says, "A lien is a public notice to your creditors that the government has a right to your current assets, including any assets you acquire after we file the lien."

This aspect of a lien may be perplexing but the confusion arises from the wording of the letter. The lien already exists by law, but filing of the lien notifies other creditors that the IRS has an interest in any property owned by a taxpayer. Even though the lien is in place, the priority rights against other creditors exists at a later time, or from the filing date of the NFTL.

The concept of priority rights means simply that the first creditor to file a lien is first in line for rights to the property.

If you have more than one creditor placing liens on your assets, the IRS takes priority usually only if they perfect their lien first. Essentially, the IRS must "take a number" like other creditors.

Of course, as with any rule, there are exceptions. For example, in states such as Texas, state statutes place their own priority right higher than the Federal government's; it doesn't matter who filed first, the state takes precedence.

Statute of Limitations for Liens

Under Federal law, IRS tax liens may expire, or become unenforceable after a certain time period.

Taxes assessed before November 5, 1990 expire in six years from the assessment date.

Taxes assessed after this date, or November 6, 1990 forward, fall under a ten-year statute of limitations, which again is the general rule. Exceptions may cause the time period to be extended.

What are some of the solutions available to solve my IRS Tax Problem?

Full Payment

If you owe money to the IRS and have received a Federal Tax Lien, wage garnishment or bank levy, there is an easy solution to your problem.

As a matter of fact, it is so easy, that sometimes I "forget" to share this strategy with my clients and prospective clients.

Let me explain.

You see, many taxpayers come to see me with various types of tax problems, things like bank levies and wage levies, that wreak havoc on their financial life.

And I begin going over all of the options available to solve their problems, including what would be the best solution for them.

As hard as it is to believe, sometimes I forget to mention the single best strategy that taxpayers can use to solve their tax problems! It is the easiest, quickest and potentially the least expensive option available.

And that option is…..

PAY OFF YOUR IRS DEBT!!!

You see, if you pay off your IRS debt, the IRS is required by law to immediately release all Federal Tax Liens, wage levies and bank levies that are in force.

Makes perfect sense, doesn't it? If you no longer owe the IRS any money, they have no right to exercise any collection activity against you or collect money from you.

It's hard to remember this option is available, as most taxpayers don't have the money to pay off their debt, or they wouldn't be coming to see me in the first place!!!

But if you do have the money, by all means, pay off the IRS and get them out of your life!

Here are some of the potholes to watch out for when paying off the IRS.

1) Is the amount the IRS says you owe correct?? Do you actually owe the tax they say you owe??
2) Did you file tax returns for the year or years in question?? If not, then it is likely that the IRS has filed one on your behalf, and the tax due is likely overstated. When the IRS prepares a return on your behalf, this is called a Substitute

for Return.
You still have the right to file a complete and accurate return, which may lower the amount of taxes, penalties and interest that you owe.

Some of the sources of funds taxpayers may consider to help them pay their taxes are:

• Cash on hand	• Checking accounts	• Savings accounts
• Money market accounts	• Borrowing on credit cards	• Borrowing from family
• Borrowing from friends	• Selling extra cars	• Selling boat
• Selling vacation home	• Borrowing from 401-K	• Working overtime
• Turning hobby to profit	• Holding a garage sale	• Selling items on Ebay
• Taking a second job	• Giving up hobbies	• Getting a raise at work

Installment Agreement

Installment agreements are perhaps the most widely used method for paying past tax debts.

If you cannot afford to pay your tax liability in full all at one time, the IRS may enter into an installment agreement with you. This will allow you to pay off your tax liability through monthly payments or installments.

Installment agreements may account for paying all (full pay) or a partial amount (partial pay) of your past tax liability.

First, we will discuss **full pay** installment agreements. This means that the monthly payments made will completely pay off the tax debt by the expiration of the statute of limitations.

If you cannot pay the amount you owe within 60 months, you must file Form 433-A or 433-B. Form 433-A (Collection Information Statement for Wage Earners and Self-Employed Individuals) is used by individual taxpayers, including self-employed taxpayers, operating as a sole proprietorship. Form 433-B (Collection Information Statement for Businesses) is used by businesses that are operating a form of business other than a sole proprietorship such as a corporation or partnership.

The IRS will analyze these forms and use the information to determine the amount they think you can afford to pay on a monthly basis.

The IRS has the discretion to decide on the payment amount and will usually negotiate with you in good faith.

The IRS will consider your financial situation and assets while negotiating with you.

You may not be approved for an installment agreement if you have money or assets that the IRS deems unnecessary to live on.

The IRS will usually inform you within 30 days whether or not your request has been accepted or denied or if you are required to submit any additional information.

If the IRS approves your request, you will be required to pay a one-time fee of $105 for establishing an Installment Agreement.

Requirements for Receiving an Installment Agreement

- You must be current on all your tax returns.
- You must make all quarterly estimated tax payments, on time, for the current year, if they are required.

- If self-employed, you must be current on your quarterly estimated tax payments for the current year.
- If you have employees, you must be current on your payroll tax and Form 941 filings.
- You must make all installment payments on time.
- You must also file all tax returns and make all tax payments including any estimated tax payments or Federal Tax Deposits during the term of the agreement on time.

Ongoing Penalties and Interest

Once you have been approved for an installment agreement, interest and penalties continue to accrue on the unpaid portion of accrued tax liability throughout the duration of the installment agreement until the tax debt is completely paid off.

The interest rate is adjusted quarterly and, combined with penalties, the rate is about 12% per year. In most cases, you could end up paying more than what you owed at the beginning.

You will be charged interest and a late payment tax penalty by the IRS on the tax not paid by April 15th, even if your request to pay tax in installments is granted by the IRS.

Effect on Enforced Collection Activities

Once you enter into an installment agreement, the IRS will suspend all collection efforts and will stop issuing wage garnishments, bank levies and notices.

Depending on the circumstances, the IRS may file a Notice of Federal Tax Lien to protect its interest until the under the terms of the Installment Agreement you have paid the liability in full.

Installment Agreement-Partial Pay

All of the requirements for receiving a Partial-Pay Installment Agreement are the same as those for a Full Pay Installment Agreement.

The only difference is that the dollar amount of payments to be made will not fully pay off the tax liability, given the remaining statute of limitations.

Each tax year may potentially have its own statute of limitations, which typically happens if tax returns are filed on time, in the year they are due.

When you make payments on any IRS tax debt, unless you state otherwise, the payment is usually assigned to the oldest debt first.

Through a combination of time remaining on the statute and the amount of money you are required to pay based upon your financial situation, there may be "less money than statute" remaining. Any balance still remaining unpaid at the end of the statute must be written off by the IRS. No further collection activity can occur on that year's debt.

Currently Not Collectible Status

If it is determined by the IRS that collecting a tax debt would pose an undue hardship on the taxpayer, based upon their monthly income, expenses and family size, the IRS may determine that it would be inequitable to pursue further collection activity with a particular taxpayer and declare them "Currently Not Collectible."

Having your account declared "Currently Not Collectible" does not eliminate the tax debt. It simply halts the collection activity for the present time.

While your account is classified as Currently Not Collectible Status, the IRS is prohibited from pursuing any enforced collection activities such as Wage or Bank Levies.

The IRS may re-evaluate and likely will evaluate this status if the taxpayer's situation changes in the future (e.g., increased income or change in marital status or family size). This strategy is most effective when coupled with the following option.

Statute of Limitations

The IRS does not have forever to collect a tax debt.

Generally, after a tax debt has been assessed, the IRS has only 10 years to collect a tax debt.

An assessment is made by filing the return, either voluntarily by the taxpayer or involuntarily by the IRS, in what is known as a Substitute for Return or SFR.

The 10-year statute is extended for the time which a taxpayer is in bankruptcy proceedings or during the time that an Offer in Compromise is pending.

After 10 years, the IRS tax debt must be written off and any associated Federal Tax Liens must be released.

Offer in Compromise

If you are unable to pay your taxes, the IRS may allow you to make an "Offer in Compromise" (OIC) to settle your tax bill.

The IRS has the discretion to accept less than the full amount of taxes owed by you if:

1) There is a doubt as to your liability – do you actually owe the taxes?

When there is doubt as to your liability, the amount of tax owed is not considered and so a payment of $100 could possibly extinguish a tax liability of $100,000.

2) There is doubt as to collectability – you do not have resources to pay the amount owed.

When there is doubt as to collectability, the IRS will conduct an analysis of your assets and earning capacity.

3) You must demonstrate that collection of the tax will create an economic hardship or will be unfair and inequitable.

This is known as effective tax administration and can be difficult to get approved.

Making an offer in compromise may be a way to solve your tax debt.

When you make an offer, you are in effect offering to pay less than the full amount of the taxes owed by you.

If you are unable to pay your taxes in full, there are other payment options, such as monthly installment agreements, that **must** be explored before an offer in compromise can be submitted.

An offer will be considered by the IRS only after other payment options have been exhausted.

Not all offers are accepted by the IRS.

Some of the reasons that your offer may not be accepted are:

1. You do not qualify for an offer, based upon the financial information submitted.

2. You did not submit the required 20% of the offer amount as the down payment which is necessary with the submission of the offer. For example, if the offer amount is $1,000, a $200 payment must be sent in with your Offer in Compromise application.

3. Your documentation was incomplete.

The IRS will not process your submitted offer if you are currently in bankruptcy, or if you have not filed all required tax returns.

It generally takes 6 months to a year for the IRS to process an offer in compromise.

Of course the idea of not having to pay a tax balance is appealing, but not everyone qualifies for an offer. Unfortunately, there are many companies out there that prey on your ignorance about the offer in compromise program.

Beware of companies that say you qualify to settle your debt for "pennies on the dollar" without gathering any detailed financial information about your situation. This could be a warning sign of an unscrupulous tax firm.

How to File an Offer in Compromise

To make an offer in compromise, you must fill out the Offer in Compromise Form 656 along with the collection information statement Form 433-A.

You must calculate your offer amount using the Form 433-A Worksheet. You must also pay a fee of $150 and make a 20 percent payment in case of a lump sum offer, or the first installment payment on a periodic payment offer.

If you are low income and meet the financial requirements, the IRS will waive this fee and initial payment requirements if you submit Form 656-A. For example, if your monthly income is less than $2,750 with a family size of 2, you would be exempt from the application fee.

Your offer must be submitted to the appropriate IRS Service Center having jurisdiction over your state.

You will be required to submit three to six months of bank statements, cancelled checks, and relevant contracts or leases.

The IRS calculates:

1) the net equity value of your assets – non-cash assets are valued at their quick sale value, which is generally 80% of their fair market value. Cash-type assets are valued at the cash balance and investment-type assets are valued at the fair market value.

2) excess monthly earnings - the net amount remaining (if any) after deducting necessary living expenses (as allowed by IRS minimum standards) multiplied by the appropriate number of months.

The two are then combined to arrive at the minimum acceptable offer.

When you submit an offer in compromise, you must prove that the amount you offer is either equal to or more than the Realizable Collection Potential as determined by the IRS.

When you make an offer in compromise, you are also agreeing to:

- Pay the offer amount.
- For the next five years, file your tax return and pay your taxes on time.
- Allow the IRS to keep any tax refunds, payments, and credits applied to your tax debts prior to submitting your offer in compromise.
- Allow the IRS to keep any tax refunds that would have been payable to you during the calendar year that your offer in compromise is approved.

Failure to agree to any of the above requirements could result in your offer in compromise being rejected.

The IRS will also consider equity, fairness and hardship when considering your offer.

If you are acting in good faith to meet your tax obligations, the IRS may consider eliminating penalties and interest during the time your offer is under consideration.

If the IRS determines the initial offer amount to be insufficient and not reflective of the your ability to pay, you will in most instances be asked to increase the offer and submit the corresponding 20 percent payment if the offer was filed as a lump sum cash offer, or the periodic payment if the offer is a short-term or deferred payment offer.

The IRS cannot seize your property while your offer is pending and during a 30-day period after an offer is rejected.

If your offer is rejected, you can appeal to the IRS Office of Appeals. If the rejected offer is appealed, no enforced collection activity can occur while the appeal is under consideration.

Filing an offer in compromise is a complicated and sometimes confusing process, but if your situation reveals that you are a good candidate (and clearly, not everyone is), it is well worth the effort to file an offer in compromise.

Bankruptcy

Filing for bankruptcy can eliminate some but not all types of IRS debt.

There are three types of bankruptcy available for individuals to file under.

Chapter 7 bankruptcy, is also known as a "liquidating" bankruptcy. Chapter 11 and Chapter 13 bankruptcies are known as "reorganizing" bankruptcies.

In some cases, under Chapter 7 bankruptcy certain taxes, penalties and interest may be discharged. "Discharged" means that the tax debt will be eliminated and that you will not have any further obligation to pay them.

In a Chapter 11 or 13 bankruptcy, there may be an option of paying the taxes due in a court-approved payment plan over three to five years. This option depends upon the ability of a taxpayer to pay the debt.

Many people believe that if they file for bankruptcy, they will not be held accountable for taxes owed either personally, or by their business. This is not true. Payroll tax liabilities incurred from the operation of a business are not dischargeable.

As soon as you file for bankruptcy, you have the protection of the automatic stay of collection activities. This applies to both the IRS and any other creditors, such as credit card companies.

Automatic stay of collection activities means that all collection actions must stop. Any levies on your bank account or any garnishments are released. Liens that were filed before the bankruptcy survive the filing on existing assets, but cannot be applied to future property or assets.

Despite this relief, the ramifications of declaring bankruptcy can be damaging. Bankruptcy is not only an expensive alternative to paying your tax, but it also may have severe negative consequences for the taxpayer's credit.

Bankruptcy may cause your credit score to go down, which may make the financing for anything, such as a home or a car, harder to get. Additionally, even when financing is secured, you may be required to make a larger down payment, and pay a higher rate of interest.

The rules for getting tax relief under bankruptcy law are rather complicated but basically they are:

- The tax return in regard to which relief is being sought was <u>filed</u> more than two years before the bankruptcy filing.

- The tax return was due more than three years before the bankruptcy filing.
- The tax liability was assessed more than 240 days before the bankruptcy filing.
- The taxpayer did not file a fraudulent tax return or engage in tax fraud.
- A tax return was actually filed for the delinquent tax liability.

Filing for bankruptcy to avoid paying taxes is a big step and should not be undertaken unless all other available options have been exhausted.

Interest Waiver

In some instances it may be possible to have the IRS remove interest that they are charging on your account. The rules are very specific.

Generally, they are 1) The IRS gave you bad advice, either written or over the phone. The burden of proof is on you to show that the IRS gave you incorrect information; and
2) There was an unusual delay by the IRS in processing your tax returns or other financial information, causing additional interest to be incurred.

Collection Due Process (CDP) Hearing

Once you receive Letter 1058, the most effective weapon you have to stop the IRS is to file Form 12153 – "Request for Collection Due Process Hearing" within 30 days from the date of the letter.

Filing this request means that the IRS has to cease collection activities immediately and wait until thirty days past the end of the Collection Due Process Hearing to confiscate assets.

The CDP hearing can happen in a month or two, but may take as long as three to six months and can provide much needed relief from IRS collections. There are only rare exceptions to this rule.

If your request for a Collection Due Process hearing is made timely, the IRS will schedule a hearing. In your request for a hearing, you must suggest an alternative option, other than a levy or lien, that would be acceptable to the IRS. For example, you can submit an Offer in Compromise or request an Installment Agreement.

The CDP hearing is presided over by an Appeals Officer who is independent from the IRS collection personnel. The purpose of the hearing is to determine whether the collection activity by the IRS is appropriate.

At the hearing, the Appeals Officer must first verify that the IRS followed all administrative and procedural requirements.

The Appeals Officer next needs to determine if the proposed IRS collection action is reasonable. Has the IRS balanced the need for efficient collection of taxes with proper consideration for the taxpayer? Has the IRS evaluated all less intrusive collection alternatives such as an Offer in Compromise or an Installment Agreement which you may have submitted with the Request for CDP Hearing?

In addition to proposing other ways to resolve your tax liability, you can also contest your liability for the underlying tax. You can only consider this option if your tax liability has not been the subject of a previous Appeals Office determination or a final Tax Court decision.

If you fail to resolve your problem at the hearing the IRS will issue a Notice of Determination.

Unless you file a lawsuit in the United States District Court, thirty days after the Notice of Determination has been issued the IRS can once again begin enforced collection activities, and levy your wages and property.

Filing for a Collection Due Process hearing and/or a lawsuit in the United States District Court also extends the 10 year statute of limitation for recovery of taxes due, for the period from when you request a hearing until 30 days after the hearing is held.

Equivalent Hearing

If the deadline for requesting a CDP Hearing has passed, you may still request an equivalent hearing using the same form you file for the standard CDP Hearing, Form 12153 – "Request for Collection Due Process Hearing."

This "equivalent hearing," while giving you the opportunity to present your case to an Appeals Officer, does not afford you the same benefits as if you had filed the request on time. The major difference between a Collection Due Process Hearing and an Equivalency Hearing is that enforced collection activity may still occur under an Equivalency Hearing.

Thus, the IRS may still levy your assets while you are awaiting the equivalency hearing. In addition, there is no right of appeal in any court against the decision of the IRS in an equivalency hearing. Despite these severe restrictions, this may be a good alternative if you missed the deadline for a Collection Due Process Hearing.

Unlike a normal Collection Due Process hearing, the equivalent hearing does not extend the 10-year statute of limitation for collection of tax debts.

Do I Even Need a Tax Professional to Solve My IRS Tax Problem?

In some instances, it may be possible to solve your IRS Tax Problem by yourself, if you want to.

These situations would include those in which:

1) the balance due is small and can be paid off in full.

If the amount the IRS says that you owe is a relatively small amount which you feel is correctly stated, then it would be advisable to pay the balance off, as soon as possible.

Things to consider: a) Were you given credit for all tax payments made, and b) Were payments credited to the proper period?

If you were not given credit for tax payments, your balance due may be overstated.

If you were not given credit for the proper period, you may be incurring higher interest and penalties than has been calculated.

If you are confident that the IRS has correctly stated the amount of tax due, including posting all tax payments paid and posting them to the proper period, then you do not need professional help.

2) All of your tax returns are filed. If you have not filed all of your tax returns, the IRS may have prepared a tax return for you and overstated your tax.

Filing all of your unfiled tax returns is one of the requirements for ALL of the solutions available from the IRS to solve your tax problems.

If you feel comfortable in preparing and filing your taxes for prior periods, including obtaining necessary tax forms and researching and understanding tax laws in effect at that time, you do not need professional help.

However, some people would just plain prefer not to deal directly with the IRS. Many taxpayers are not interested in or are just extremely uncomfortable with dealing with or negotiating with the IRS. Perhaps they have had prior dealings with the IRS that left a bad taste in their mouth. Or perhaps they don't have the time or just don't feel like dealing with a government bureaucracy.

If you are one of those people, getting the help of a tax professional will be your best strategy.
What Types of Tax Professionals are Available to Help Solve My IRS Tax Problem?

Enrolled Agents (EAs): Enrolled Agents are individuals who have passed an examination administered by the IRS. This test covers only tax matters. The IRS is the sanctioning body and licenses individuals as enrolled agents.

Enrolled Agents are frequently ex-IRS employees and receive their EA status by virtue of their employment with the IRS.

There is no particular educational requirement to be an Enrolled Agent. Former employment with the IRS or passing the Enrolled Agent's exam are the only criteria for being named an Enrolled Agent.

Attorney: Attorneys are automatically licensed to practice before the IRS by virtue of their attorney status. No additional specialized tax knowledge or tax experience is required.

Attorneys at a minimum must have a four-year undergraduate degree, as well as a law school degree.

CPAs (Certified Public Accountants): CPAs are tax and financial professionals who have passed a rigorous 2½-day national examination. CPAs must have an undergraduate college degree and train directly under the supervision of another CPA for at least 2 years.

All CPAs are commonly thought of by the general public as experts in tax matters. Nothing could be further from the truth.

Many CPAs spend their entire careers doing accounting work for businesses large and small, or they work in public accounting firms, doing audits of publicly-held companies.

And some of these CPAs would be hard-pressed to even do their own tax returns. Okay, that may be a bit harsh, but they don't work in the tax area and they don't keep current with changing tax laws or prepare any tax returns but their own.

That said, I do think that a CPA would be the best choice to solve your IRS tax problem – but not just any CPA. Some CPAs work with taxes, and some don't prepare taxes but work in financial accounting. But not all of the CPAs who spend their time preparing taxes have any experience at all in working with the IRS solving tax problems.

Most CPAs with tax practices have clients who come to them for tax preparation. These clients have their taxes prepared, file them and either get a refund or have a small balance due, which they then pay. (Hopefully, the client and CPA working together have done some tax planning to minimize their taxes, or calculated the amount of money needed for estimated tax payments and made those tax payments –

either way resulting in no balance due or just a small tax balance due.)

In order to get the best possible results, I would advise you to choose a CPA with specific IRS Tax Problem Solving experience who also has the following qualities:

1) **Extensive tax preparation experience.** Many taxpayers with tax problems have not filed their tax returns for a number of years, and need the services of professionals who are well-versed in taxes for the time periods the taxpayers didn't file.

Ideally, a CPA should have 10 years of solid tax preparation experience, at a minimum. This experience ensures that they know the tax laws for those past years, because they have already prepared numerous tax returns for those years. These CPAs won't have to go and look up the applicable tax law for those years.

2) **Accounting experience.** Most CPAs have a solid accounting background, even if they have worked with taxes their entire careers.

Many taxpayers own small businesses and need some type of guidance and assistance in pulling together their records, commonly a statement of Profit and Loss, detailing what their income is.

A CPA with solid accounting experience can be invaluable in helping compile the information needed to file a complete and accurate return.

3) **Experience across various industries.** A CPA who has been practicing for a while has typically worked with clients in many different businesses and industries. Every business and industry is unique, with its own challenges. Having a CPA with varied accounting and tax experience will be invaluable in working to identify accounting and tax issues specific to your business.

4) **Tax planning experience.** Even if you have IRS Tax Problems, the name of the game is to lower your taxes, whenever possible.

If there are tax returns that will need to be completed, there may still be some tax-saving opportunities available to implement, even if they are somewhat limited.

And lowering your taxes will lower the total balance that you owe the IRS, including any penalties and interest.

About My Practice

I personally work on all cases myself. While I have an assistant, all of the contact between my clients and my office is directly with me.

I will be responsible for analyzing your situation and determining the best strategy for us to implement. I will personally speak with and negotiate with the IRS myself.

If I decide to accept your case, I will almost always quote a FLAT FEE so that you know exactly what the cost will be from the start of the case until we are finished.

I am a consumer as well, and do not employ the *"just give me a blank check and I'll tell you how much it will be when it's finished"* approach.

I have been doing this for a long time and I know how much time it will take to work on your case, so I can quote a fixed fee that's fair.

There are a small number of cases for which I will not be able to quote a fixed fee due to their unusual degree of uncertainty, but I will tell you this upfront. This happens rarely.

You can rest assured that unlike some of the National Tax Resolution Firms out there, if I say I am going to get you a particular solution (installment agreement, or whatever it may be), that is the solution that *I will* get for you. There will be no surprises.

The Types of Cases I Accept

I am able to accept a few new cases to work on every month.

I work hard to settle cases for my clients as quickly as possible, and to obtain the best solution at the least cost to my clients. I am an advocate for my clients and their rights, and I represent them vigorously.

It makes no difference what caused the taxpayer to find themselves with a tax problem. I'm non-judgmental about that. I know that most taxpayers don't just wake up one morning and decide that they aren't going to pay the IRS anymore.

Typically, something unfortunate happened in their life which started the problem and led them to where they are now.

It's my job to help them get back on track, remove the stress associated with dealing with the IRS, and help return life back to a sense of normalcy.

I am interested in working with taxpayers who are ready to move forward. Talking about what caused the problem in the first place doesn't really help to solve the problem.

However, taking action and moving forward *does* help to fix the problem. I need clients to work together with me, as partners, to solve their problem. We are truly on the same team.

Any documents that I request, I'll need to receive as soon as possible to complete your case. And if I ask for documents, it's not because I need a bunch of extra paper cluttering up your file. Any papers I need are for documentation purposes, in order to get the best result possible for you. And again – I would need the documents as soon as possible, so that we can keep your case moving forward to completion.

Many times, I will have already spoken to your Revenue Officer and committed to a deadline for providing information, and it is better for both of us to honor our time commitments.

Another requirement that I have for my clients is that they must be totally honest with me.

It makes it much more difficult to resolve your case, when in the course of negotiation with the IRS, I find out that the facts are different than I know them to be.

Not only does this endanger us obtaining the solution that we were striving for – it makes us both look bad in the eyes of the IRS/Revenue Officer, which in turn makes it harder to deal with them.

If you are tired of receiving those pesky IRS notices, or have received a levy on your paycheck or bank account, give me a call. If I have time in my schedule, I will be very happy to discuss your case with you.

The Types of Cases I Don't Accept

I enjoy working with taxpayers to help them solve their IRS Tax Problems. The sense of relief that my clients experience as we head to a resolution makes my work so worthwhile.

But there are two types of client situations for which I will not accept an engagement.

The first of those is in the case of taxpayers who claim that the income tax is illegal and that the IRS does not have the right to tax income.

Many frivolous and false arguments have been made over the years, and all have resulted in the taxpayer losing their arguments and suffering the negative consequences.

Working with the IRS can be challenging enough. It is simply counterproductive, for my clients and myself, to have to be in the position of constantly arguing with my clients over the legality of the income tax. Therefore, I cannot accept that kind of case.

Another type of client situation I cannot engage in is when the taxpayers themselves are not really ready to solve their problem. Many people give lip service to wanting to solve their tax problem, even going so far as wanting to retain me to work on the case.

In many cases, however, I will need the taxpayer to furnish additional information to put together documentation to solve the case. And if the taxpayer is not ready or not willing to provide the information, the case comes to a stand-still.

This can be frustrating for the IRS, for the taxpayer, and quite frankly can be frustrating for me, because I am not able to represent my client in the best possible manner.

So if either of these above situations describe you, please don't call!

Glossary of Terms

ACS (Automated Collection Service) - A branch of the IRS that is involved with collection of tax due. Most of the contact from the IRS will be by mail, to your last known address, but the IRS might also contact you by phone.

Back Taxes - Taxes owed from a previous period or year that a taxpayer did not pay when due, either accidentally or intentionally. Back taxes may also arise when taxes are underpaid. Individuals may avoid penalties and fines by filing back taxes accurately and expeditiously.

Bank Levy - A Notice of Levy is sent to the taxpayer's bank and attaches to all accounts in the name of the taxpayer, regardless of whether a sole or joint account. Banks are legally obligated to honor the levy. A bank levy freezes the funds on deposit in the account, and the bank cannot allow anyone access to the frozen funds for 21 days from the date of receipt of the levy. If prior arrangements are not made and a "Release of Levy" has not been issued, the bank must send the frozen funds to the IRS on the 22st day.

Bankruptcy - A legal procedure that may result in debt relief. Debt relief can be obtained through either liquidating assets or reorganizing debt. This release of debt is referred to as a discharge. Bankruptcy laws are very specific about the discharge of taxes. The Internal Revenue Service can obtain relief from any protection that a bankruptcy might offer. Not all types of taxes can be discharged. Taxes can only be discharged based upon very specific parameters. Thus, it is possible to file for bankruptcy and still have a remaining tax debt.

Collection Due Process Hearing - A Hearing held with the IRS Appeals Division. The IRS will determine that all of their rules were followed before enforced collection activity was permitted. If request for a Collection Due Process hearing was filed for on a timely basis, all collection activity must stop until the Hearing is held. During the Hearing, solutions such as an Installment Agreement or Offer in Compromise may be filed.

Collection Information Forms - IRS standard financial statements required from individuals and/or self-employed individuals (Form 433-A) and businesses (Form 433-B) that owe IRS taxes and have indicated an inability to pay the liability in full. The IRS uses these forms to determine the taxpayer's ability to pay, and how much. Used for Installment Agreements, Offers in Compromise and Currently Not Collectible.

Criminal Investigation Division - A branch of the IRS that investigates cases in which the IRS suspects some type of tax fraud or illegal activities are occurring.

Currently Not Collectible Status - A situation in which the IRS recognizes the taxpayer does not currently have the ability to pay their taxes owed via full payment or through an installment agreement or Offer in Compromise. If a taxpayer's account is placed on Currently Non-Collectible status the IRS does not pursue enforced collection activity against the taxpayer. The statute of limitations on the tax liabilities continue to run. A taxpayer's account should remain in Currently Non-Collectible status, unless the taxpayer's financial situation changes for the better.

Discharge - An elimination of your tax debt. You will no longer be held responsible for paying the tax due.

Federal Tax Lien - A legal claim by the IRS against a delinquent taxpayer's property as payment of or security for back taxes. The IRS may file a tax lien after 1) it determines the individual's tax liability; 2) it sends a notice and demand for payment; and 3) the debtor fails to submit payment within 10 days of receiving the notice. When a federal tax lien is imposed on a taxpayer's property, the tax debt must be paid from the net proceeds when the asset is sold.

Installment Agreement - An IRS payment plan which allows taxpayers who are current in their tax return filings to pay off their back taxes in manageable and smaller increments. To receive an installment agreement, taxpayers must:
1) determine their tax liability; 2) set up a payment plan;

3) fix a date for their monthly payments; and 4) select a monthly payment amount.

Offer in Compromise - A tax debt settlement solution that allows a taxpayer to pay off his or her tax debt for an amount less than what he or she owes. Tax liabilities may be settled if one of the following criteria is present: 1) Doubt as to the IRS' ability to collect the tax debt; 2) Doubt as to the taxpayer's liability for the debt; or 3) Imposition of the tax would be inequitable and unfair or would pose an economic hardship to the taxpayer.

Power of Attorney - An authorization to act on someone else's behalf in a legal or business matter. The person authorizing the other to act is the principal or grantor (of the power), and the one authorized to act is the agent or CPA. To have a CPA represent you before the Internal Revenue Service you must complete an IRS Form 2848, "Power of Attorney." The individual you authorize must be a person eligible to "Practice before the IRS" (i.e., CPA, attorney, or Enrolled Agent). Your authorization allows that individual to receive and inspect your confidential tax information and act on your behalf when discussing and resolving issues with the Internal Revenue Service. The IRS will not discuss your case or release ANY of your confidential tax information without a properly signed Form 2848 "Power of Attorney" in place.

Release of Levy - A document issued by the IRS, typically either to a bank or employer, officially allowing a levy to be released (levy no longer required). The IRS will typically only do this if an acceptable solution to take care of the tax debt is put into place by the taxpayer, and accepted by the IRS.

Revenue Agent - An IRS employee whose sole job is to determine that the tax returns you file correctly state your income, expenses and taxes. Revenue agents do not typically get involved in the collection of the tax.

Revenue Officer - An IRS employee whose job is to collect the amount of tax owed to the IRS. Some of the tools at their disposal include bank and wage levies and filing of Federal Tax Liens.

Statute of Limitations - The time limit under which the IRS may collect a tax. The IRS does not have forever to collect taxes owed – Normally, the Collection Statute is 10 years from the date of assessment, but can be extended in certain situations.

Substitute for Return - A tax return prepared by the IRS on your behalf. When preparing a Substitute for Return, the IRS will gather the income information reported by the taxpayer in the form of W-2s and 1099s. After determining the taxpayer's income, the Internal Revenue Service will often prepare the return in a light least favorable to the taxpayer. For example, a 1040 filer would be filed as single or married filing separately, with no dependents or itemized deductions. If the taxpayer also had self-employment income, the Schedule C would reflect business income, but no expenses. A Substitute for Return almost always reflects a much higher tax than what the taxpayer would have been assessed, had the taxpayer filed a tax return on their own.

Wage Levy - A wage levy (also known as a wage garnishment) is a procedure in which your employer is notified and ordered to withhold money from your paycheck to pay your taxes. An employer is legally obligated to comply with the terms of the wage garnishment. Through the wage garnishment, the IRS is allowed to take all of a taxpayer's wages up to a certain threshold. The IRS gives the employer a document informing the employer of how much they can allow the employee to receive of their paycheck. Any amount above this must be remitted to the IRS. Frequently, the amount the IRS can garnish is up to 80% of a taxpayer's wages. Wage garnishments are ongoing until the taxpayer contacts the IRS and negotiates a release of the garnishment.

Unfiled return-A tax return that was not filed by the taxpayer. Even though a tax return was never filed by the taxpayer, the IRS may have prepared a tax return (Substitute for Return) and made an assessment of tax.

Frequently Asked Questions

Can the IRS really garnish my paycheck?

This is a commonly asked question. Yes, the IRS can garnish a taxpayer's paycheck. This is the last step that the IRS will typically use to "get the taxpayer's attention" and get them to deal with their IRS Tax Problem.

Before the IRS can garnish a paycheck (officially called a wage levy), they must go through their own due process. They can't just arbitrarily levy a paycheck.

The IRS must send a series of letters to the taxpayer's last known address requesting payment. The final letter in the sequence is known as the Letter 1058, Final Notice of Intent to Levy.

If the taxpayer doesn't respond within 30 days of the date of the letter and request a Collection Due Process Hearing, the IRS can then commence levy activities after 30 days have passed.

Sometimes taxpayers are surprised by a levy because they have moved numerous times and haven't received notices. Some taxpayers receive notices and either didn't open their mail, or opened their mail and didn't understand the process and the seriousness of the IRS requests. And still others received and read the notices, and chose to ignore them.

Whatever the cause, a release of levy *can* be obtained. The solution usually consists of filing ALL past due tax returns and putting a solution in place that is acceptable to the IRS, such as an Installment Agreement.

If a taxpayer receives a Wage Levy, fast action is required to keep the IRS from taking most of the taxpayer's paycheck.

I can't afford to pay the IRS what I owe them – I'm "broke"!! All the money I earn goes to pay my bills. Is there any help for me?

There is always a solution to the problem. Some solutions will be better than others.

There are a couple of options to explore. First we have to define what "being broke" is. The IRS will look at your monthly income and expenses in analyzing any of the alternatives available to solve your tax problems.

Monthly income is determined and compared to your monthly "allowable" expenses. The IRS has established maximum amounts that they will typically allow for payment of Food/Clothing/Miscellaneous, Housing/Utilities, Car

Payments, Car Expenses, Health Insurance, Other Healthcare costs, Life Insurance and Taxes.

If the amount you are paying in a particular category exceeds the amount the IRS allows, there may be a potential problem.

Some taxpayers live in expensive homes and carry big mortgages, or may have expensive cars with a large monthly car payments. These taxpayers may say that they are "broke" because their monthly income equals their monthly expenses. But not all of the expenses will be allowed by the IRS.

Situations such as these can be more difficult to solve, but they are certainly not impossible.

Bonus Report - The Truth Behind The "Pennies on the Dollar" Tax Representation Firms Finally Revealed

One of the most common questions clients and prospective clients ask me is about the "Pennies on the Dollars" deals.

You've probably seen the offers on cable TV at all hours of the day and night, offering to settle your IRS Tax Debt for only "Pennies on the Dollar."

Let's be honest here. Who wouldn't be thrilled to settle any outstanding debt you have, let alone a debt that is owed to the IRS, for less than you actually owe? Maybe even paying only a couple of cents on the dollar!

I know I sure would. Unfortunately, the promises made by many of these national firms are only that and nothing more. Promises.

The truth is that many of the taxpayers with IRS Tax Problems will not qualify for these "Pennies on the Dollar" offers.

The IRS program that these firms are making reference to is known officially as the Offer in Compromise program.

And if you qualify for an Offer in Compromise, the amount of your tax debt doesn't matter. And the good news is, it doesn't matter whether you owe $10,000 or $1 million.

Under the Offer in Compromise program, the IRS evaluates a taxpayer's financial situation, and in certain very limited circumstances, will accept an offer to settle the debt for less than is actually owed them.

The problems is that most unscrupulous "tax settlement" firms will tell a taxpayer, either over the phone or in person, that they qualify for an offer in compromise, without looking at the taxpayer's financial information to see if they actually do qualify.

It is ultimately up to the IRS to determine whether a taxpayer qualifies for an offer in compromise.

Appendix
Commonly Used IRS Collection Forms

CP 501

Reminder

We show you still owe: **{amount due}**

According to our records, you haven't paid all you owe for tax period **{date}**. To avoid additional penalty and interest, please pay the full amount you owe within ten days from the date of this notice. We can file a Notice of Federal Tax Lien if your balance owed is not paid within 10 days from the date of this notice. If you already paid your balance in full or arranged for an installment agreement, please disregard this notice.

CP 503

IMPORTANT!!

Immediate action is required.

We previously wrote to you about your unpaid account, but you haven't contacted us about it. Penalties and interest on the unpaid balance are continuing to increase. Please pay the amount you owe within ten days from the date of this notice. If you can't pay now, call us at the number shown below. You may be qualified for an installment agreement or payroll deduction agreement. We want to help you resolve this bill. However, if we don't hear from you, we will have no choice but to proceed with steps required to collect the amount you owe.

If you already paid your balance in full or arranged for an installment agreement, please disregard this notice.

CP 504

Urgent!!

We intend to levy on certain assets.
Please respond NOW.

Our records indicate that you haven't paid the amount you owe. The law requires that you pay your tax at the time you file your return. This is your notice, as required by Internal Revenue Code Section 6331(d), of our intent to levy (take) any state tax refunds that you may be entitled to if we don't receive your payment in full. In addition, we will begin to search for other assets we may levy. We can also file a Notice of Federal Tax Lien, if we haven't already done so. To prevent collection action, please pay the current balance now. If you've already paid, can't pay, or have arranged for an installment agreement, it is important that you call us immediately at the telephone number shown below.

Letter 1058-FINAL NOTICE

NOTICE OF INTENT TO LEVY AND NOTICE OF YOUR RIGHT TO A HEARING

PLEASE RESPOND IMMEDIATELY

Your Federal tax is still not paid. We previously asked you to pay this, but we still haven't received your payment. This letter is your notice of our intent to levy under Internal Revenue Code (IRC) Section 6331 and your right to receive Appeals consideration.

We may file a Notice of Federal Tax Lien at any time to protect the government's interest. A lien is a public notice to your creditors that the government has a right to your current assets, including any assets you acquire after we file the lien.

If you don't pay the amount you owe, make alternative arrangements to pay, or request Appeals consideration within 30 days from the date of this letter, we may take your property, or rights to property, such as real estate, automobiles, business assets, bank accounts, wages, commissions, and other income. We've enclosed Publication 594 with more information, Publication 1660 explaining your right to appeal, and Form 12153 to request a Collection Due Process hearing with Appeals.

To prevent collection action, please send your full payment today. Make your check or money order payable to U.S. Treasury. Write your social security number or employer identification number on your payment. Send your payment to us in the enclosed envelope with a copy of this letter.

Forms Commonly Used to Solve IRS Tax Problems

Form 8822 - Change of Address

Form **8822**
(Rev. December 2007)
Department of the Treasury
Internal Revenue Service

Change of Address

▶ **Please type or print.**

▶ **See instructions on back.** ▶ **Do not attach this form to your return.**

OMB No. 1545-1163

Part I **Complete This Part To Change Your Home Mailing Address**

Check **all** boxes this change affects:

1 ☐ Individual income tax returns (Forms 1040, 1040A, 1040EZ, 1040NR, etc.)
▶ If your last return was a joint return and you are now establishing a residence separate from the spouse with whom you filed that return, check here . . . . ▶ ☐

2 ☐ Gift, estate, or generation-skipping transfer tax returns (Forms 706, 709, etc.)
▶ For Forms 706 and 706-NA, enter the decedent's name and social security number below.

▶ Decedent's name ▶ Social security number

3a **Your name** (first name, initial, and last name) | 3b **Your social security number**

4a **Spouse's name** (first name, initial, and last name) | 4b **Spouse's social security number**

5 **Prior name(s).** See instructions.

6a **Old address** (no., street, city or town, state, and ZIP code). If a P.O. box or foreign address, see instructions. | Apt. no.

6b **Spouse's old address,** if different from line 6a (no., street, city or town, state, and ZIP code). If a P.O. box or foreign address, see instructions. | Apt. no.

7 **New address** (no., street, city or town, state, and ZIP code). If a P.O. box or foreign address, see instructions. | Apt. no.

Part II **Complete This Part To Change Your Business Mailing Address or Business Location**

Check **all** boxes this change affects:

8 ☐ Employment, excise, income, and other business returns (Forms 720, 940, 940-EZ, 941, 990, 1041, 1065, 1120, etc.)
9 ☐ Employee plan returns (Forms 5500, 5500-EZ, etc.)
10 ☐ Business location

11a **Business name** | 11b **Employer identification number**

12 **Old mailing address** (no., street, city or town, state, and ZIP code). If a P.O. box or foreign address, see instructions. | Room or suite no.

13 **New mailing address** (no., street, city or town, state, and ZIP code). If a P.O. box or foreign address, see instructions. | Room or suite no.

14 **New business location** (no., street, city or town, state, and ZIP code). If a foreign address, see instructions. | Room or suite no.

Part III **Signature**

Daytime telephone number of person to contact (optional) ▶ ( )

Sign Here
▶ Your signature | Date
▶ If Part II completed, signature of owner, officer, or representative | Date
▶ If joint return, spouse's signature | Date
▶ Title

For Privacy Act and Paperwork Reduction Act Notice, see back of form. Cat. No. 12081V Form **8822** (Rev. 12-2007)

Form 8822 - Change of Address (cont.)

Purpose of Form

You can use Form 8822 to notify the Internal Revenue Service if you changed your home or business mailing address or your business location. If this change also affects the mailing address for your children who filed income tax returns, complete and file a separate Form 8822 for each child. If you are a representative signing for the taxpayer, attach to Form 8822 a copy of your power of attorney.

Changing both home and business addresses? If you are, use a separate Form 8822 to show each change.

Prior Name(s)

If you or your spouse changed your name because of marriage, divorce, etc., complete line 5. Also, be sure to notify the Social Security Administration of your new name so that it has the same name in its records that you have on your tax return. This prevents delays in processing your return and issuing refunds. It also safeguards your future social security benefits.

Addresses

Be sure to include any apartment, room, or suite number in the space provided.

P.O. Box

Enter your box number instead of your street address only if your post office does not deliver mail to your street address.

Foreign Address

Enter the information in the following order: city, province or state, and country. Follow the country's practice for entering the postal code. Please do not abbreviate the country name.

"In Care of" Address

If you receive your mail in care of a third party (such as an accountant or attorney), enter "C/O" followed by the third party's name and street address or P.O. box.

Signature

If you are completing Part I, the taxpayer, executor, donor, or an authorized representative must sign. If your last return was a joint return, your spouse must also sign (unless you have indicated by checking the box on line 1 that you are establishing a separate residence).

If you are completing Part II, an officer, owner, general partner or LLC member manager, plan administrator, fiduciary, or an authorized representative must sign. An officer is the president, vice president, treasurer, chief accounting officer, etc.

CAUTION *If you are a representative signing on behalf of the taxpayer, you must attach to Form 8822 a copy of your power of attorney. To do this, you can use Form 2848. The Internal Revenue Service will not complete an address change from an "unauthorized" third party.*

Where To File

Send this form to the Department of the Treasury, Internal Revenue Service Center, and the address shown next that applies to you. Generally, it takes 4 to 6 weeks to process your change of address.

Note. If you checked the box on line 2, or you checked the box on both lines 1 and 2, send this form to: Cincinnati, OH 45999-0023.

Filers Who Completed Part I (You checked the box on line 1 only)

IF your old home mailing address was in . . .	THEN use this address . . .
District of Columbia, Maine, Maryland, Massachusetts, New Hampshire, New York, Vermont	Andover, MA 05501-0023
Alabama, Delaware, Florida, Georgia, North Carolina, Rhode Island, South Carolina, Virginia	Atlanta, GA 39901-0023
Kentucky, Louisiana, Mississippi, Tennessee, Texas, APO, FPO	Austin, TX 73301-0023
Alaska, Arizona, California, Colorado, Hawaii, Idaho, Iowa, Kansas, Minnesota, Montana, Nebraska, Nevada, New Mexico, North Dakota, Oklahoma, Oregon, South Dakota, Utah, Washington, Wisconsin, Wyoming	Fresno, CA 93888-0023
Arkansas, Connecticut, Illinois, Indiana, Michigan, Missouri, New Jersey, Ohio, Pennsylvania, West Virginia	Kansas City, MO 64999-0023
American Samoa Guam: Nonpermanent residents Puerto Rico (or if excluding income under Internal Revenue Code section 933) Virgin Islands: Nonpermanent residents Nonresident aliens and dual-status aliens Foreign country: U.S. citizens and those filing Form 2555, Form 2555-EZ, or Form 4563	Austin, TX 73301-0023 USA
Guam: Permanent residents	Department of Revenue and Taxation Government of Guam P.O. Box 23607 GMF, GU 96921
Virgin Islands: Permanent residents	V.I. Bureau of Internal Revenue 9601 Estate Thomas Charlotte Amalie St. Thomas, VI 00802

Filers Who Completed Part II

IF your old business address was in . . .	THEN use this address . . .
Connecticut, Delaware, District of Columbia, Illinois, Indiana, Kentucky, Maine, Maryland, Massachusetts, Michigan, New Hampshire, New Jersey, New York, North Carolina, Ohio, Pennsylvania, Rhode Island, South Carolina, Vermont, Virginia, West Virginia, Wisconsin	Cincinnati, OH 45999-0023
Alabama, Alaska, Arizona, Arkansas, California, Colorado, Florida, Georgia, Hawaii, Idaho, Iowa, Kansas, Louisiana, Minnesota, Mississippi, Missouri, Montana, Nebraska, Nevada, New Mexico, North Dakota, Oklahoma, Oregon, South Dakota, Tennessee, Texas, Utah, Washington, Wyoming, any place outside the United States	Ogden, UT 84201-0023

Privacy Act and Paperwork Reduction Act Notice. We ask for the information on this form to carry out the Internal Revenue laws of the United States. We may give the information to the Department of Justice and to other federal agencies, as provided by law. We may give it to cities, states, the District of Columbia, and U.S. common- wealths or possessions to carry out their tax laws. We may also disclose this information to other countries under a tax treaty, to federal and state agencies to enforce federal nontax criminal laws, or to federal law enforcement and intelligence agencies to combat terrorism.

Our legal right to ask for information is Internal Revenue Code sections 6001 and 6011, which require you to file a statement with us for any tax for which you are liable. Section 6109 requires that you provide your social security number on what you file. This is so we know who you are, and can process your form and other papers.

You are not required to provide the information requested on a form that is subject to the Paperwork Reduction Act unless the form displays a valid OMB control number. Books or records relating to a form or its instructions must be retained as long as their contents may become material in the administration of any Internal Revenue law. Generally, tax returns and return information are confidential, as required by section 6103.

The use of this form is voluntary. However, if you fail to provide the Internal Revenue Service with your current mailing address, you may not receive a notice of deficiency or a notice and demand for tax. Despite the failure to receive such notices, penalties and interest will continue to accrue on the tax deficiencies.

The time needed to complete and file this form will vary depending on individual circumstances. The estimated burden for individual taxpayers filing this form is approved under OMB control number 1545-0074 and is included in the estimates shown in the instructions for their individual income tax return. The estimated burden for all other taxpayers who file this form is 16 minutes.

If you have comments concerning the accuracy of this time estimate or suggestions for making this form simpler, we would be happy to hear from you. You can write to the Internal Revenue Service, Tax Products Coordinating Committee, SE:W:CAR:MP:T:T:SP, 1111 Constitution Ave. NW, IR-6526, Washington, DC 20224. Do not send the form to this address. Instead, see *Where To File* on this page.

Form 2848 - Power of Attorney

Form **2848**
(Rev. June 2008)
Department of the Treasury
Internal Revenue Service

Power of Attorney
and Declaration of Representative
▶ **Type or print.** ▶ **See the separate instructions.**

OMB No. 1545-0150
For IRS Use Only
Received by:
Name
Telephone
Function
Date / /

Part I **Power of Attorney**

Caution: *Form 2848 will not be honored for any purpose other than representation before the IRS.*

1 **Taxpayer information.** Taxpayer(s) must sign and date this form on page 2, line 9.

Taxpayer name(s) and address	**Social security number(s)**	**Employer identification number**
	Daytime telephone number ( )	Plan number (if applicable)

hereby appoint(s) the following representative(s) as attorney(s)-in-fact:

2 **Representative(s)** must sign and date this form on page 2, Part II.

Name and address	CAF No. Telephone No. Fax No. Check if new: Address ☐ Telephone No. ☐ Fax No. ☐
Name and address	CAF No. Telephone No. Fax No. Check if new: Address ☐ Telephone No. ☐ Fax No. ☐
Name and address	CAF No. Telephone No. Fax No. Check if new: Address ☐ Telephone No. ☐ Fax No. ☐

to represent the taxpayer(s) before the Internal Revenue Service for the following tax matters:

3 **Tax matters**

Type of Tax (Income, Employment, Excise, etc.) or Civil Penalty (see the instructions for line 3)	Tax Form Number (1040, 941, 720, etc.)	Year(s) or Period(s) (see the instructions for line 3)

4 **Specific use not recorded on Centralized Authorization File (CAF).** If the power of attorney is for a specific use not recorded on CAF, check this box. See the instructions for **Line 4. Specific Uses Not Recorded on CAF** . . . . ▶ ☐

5 **Acts authorized.** The representatives are authorized to receive and inspect confidential tax information and to perform any and all acts that I (we) can perform with respect to the tax matters described on line 3, for example, the authority to sign any agreements, consents, or other documents. The authority does not include the power to receive refund checks (see line 6 below), the power to substitute another representative or add additional representatives, the power to sign certain returns, or the power to execute a request for disclosure of tax returns or return information to a third party. See the line 5 instructions for more information.

Exceptions. An unenrolled return preparer cannot sign any document for a taxpayer and may only represent taxpayers in limited situations. See **Unenrolled Return Preparer** on page 1 of the instructions. An enrolled actuary may only represent taxpayers to the extent provided in section 10.3(d) of Treasury Department Circular No. 230 (Circular 230). An enrolled retirement plan administrator may only represent taxpayers to the extent provided in section 10.3(e) of Circular 230. See the line 5 instructions for restrictions on tax matters partners. In most cases, the student practitioner's (levels k and l) authority is limited (for example, they may only practice under the supervision of another practitioner).

List any specific additions or deletions to the acts otherwise authorized in this power of attorney: ....

6 **Receipt of refund checks.** If you want to authorize a representative named on line 2 to receive, **BUT NOT TO ENDORSE OR CASH**, refund checks, initial here ________ and list the name of that representative below.

Name of representative to receive refund check(s) ▶

For Privacy Act and Paperwork Reduction Act Notice, see page 4 of the instructions. Cat. No. 11980J Form **2848** (Rev. 6-2008)

Form 2848 - Power of Attorney (cont.)

Form 2848 (Rev. 6-2008) Page **2**

7 Notices and communications. Original notices and other written communications will be sent to you and a copy to the first representative listed on line 2.

a If you also want the second representative listed to receive a copy of notices and communications, check this box . . . . . . ▶ ☐

b If you do not want any notices or communications sent to your representative(s), check this box . . . . ▶ ☐

8 Retention/revocation of prior power(s) of attorney. The filing of this power of attorney automatically revokes all earlier power(s) of attorney on file with the Internal Revenue Service for the same tax matters and years or periods covered by this document. If you **do not** want to revoke a prior power of attorney, check here . . . . ▶ ☐

YOU MUST ATTACH A COPY OF ANY POWER OF ATTORNEY YOU WANT TO REMAIN IN EFFECT.

9 Signature of taxpayer(s). If a tax matter concerns a joint return, **both** husband and wife must sign if joint representation is requested, otherwise, see the instructions. If signed by a corporate officer, partner, guardian, tax matters partner, executor, receiver, administrator, or trustee on behalf of the taxpayer, I certify that I have the authority to execute this form on behalf of the taxpayer.

▶ **IF NOT SIGNED AND DATED, THIS POWER OF ATTORNEY WILL BE RETURNED.**

Signature .... Date .... Title (if applicable) ....

Print Name .... ☐☐☐☐☐ PIN Number .... Print name of taxpayer from line 1 if other than individual

Signature .... Date .... Title (if applicable) ....

Print Name .... ☐☐☐☐☐ PIN Number

Part II Declaration of Representative

Caution: *Students with a special order to represent taxpayers in qualified Low Income Taxpayer Clinics or the Student Tax Clinic Program (levels k and l), see the instructions for Part II.*

Under penalties of perjury, I declare that:

- I am not currently under suspension or disbarment from practice before the Internal Revenue Service;
- I am aware of regulations contained in Circular 230 (31 CFR, Part 10), as amended, concerning the practice of attorneys, certified public accountants, enrolled agents, enrolled actuaries, and others;
- I am authorized to represent the taxpayer(s) identified in Part I for the tax matter(s) specified there; and
- I am one of the following:

a Attorney—a member in good standing of the bar of the highest court of the jurisdiction shown below.

b Certified Public Accountant—duly qualified to practice as a certified public accountant in the jurisdiction shown below.

c Enrolled Agent—enrolled as an agent under the requirements of Circular 230.

d Officer—a bona fide officer of the taxpayer's organization.

e Full-Time Employee—a full-time employee of the taxpayer.

f Family Member—a member of the taxpayer's immediate family (for example, spouse, parent, child, brother, or sister).

g Enrolled Actuary—enrolled as an actuary by the Joint Board for the Enrollment of Actuaries under 29 U.S.C. 1242 (the authority to practice before the Internal Revenue Service is limited by section 10.3(d) of Circular 230).

h Unenrolled Return Preparer—the authority to practice before the Internal Revenue Service is limited by Circular 230, section 10.7(c)(1)(viii). You must have prepared the return in question and the return must be under examination by the IRS. See **Unenrolled Return Preparer** on page 1 of the instructions.

k Student Attorney—student who receives permission to practice before the IRS by virtue of their status as a law student under section 10.7(d) of Circular 230.

l Student CPA—student who receives permission to practice before the IRS by virtue of their status as a CPA student under section 10.7(d) of Circular 230.

r Enrolled Retirement Plan Agent—enrolled as a retirement plan agent under the requirements of Circular 230 (the authority to practice before the Internal Revenue Service is limited by section 10.3(e)).

▶ **IF THIS DECLARATION OF REPRESENTATIVE IS NOT SIGNED AND DATED, THE POWER OF ATTORNEY WILL BE RETURNED.** See the Part II instructions.

Designation—Insert above letter (a–r)	Jurisdiction (state) or identification	Signature	Date

Form **2848** (Rev. 6-2008)

Form 433-A - Collection Information Statement for Wage Earners and Self-Employed Individuals

Form **433-A**
(Rev. January 2008)
Department of the Treasury
Internal Revenue Service

Collection Information Statement for Wage Earners and Self-Employed Individuals

Wage Earners Complete Sections 1, 2, 3, and 4, including signature line on page 4. *Answer all questions or write N/A.*
Self-Employed Individuals Complete Sections 1, 2, 3, 4, 5 and 6 and signature line on page 4. *Answer all questions or write N/A.*
For Additional Information, refer to Publication 1854, "How To Prepare a Collection Information Statement"
Include attachments if additional space is needed to respond completely to any question.

Name on Internal Revenue Service (IRS) Account	Social Security Number SSN on IRS Account	Employer Identification Number EIN

Section 1: Personal Information

1a Full Name of Taxpayer and Spouse (if applicable)	1c Home Phone ( )	1d Cell Phone ( )
1b Address *(Street, City, State, ZIP code) (County of Residence)*	1e Business Phone ( )	1f Business Cell Phone ( )
	2b Name, Age, and Relationship of dependent(s)	
2a Marital Status: ☐ Married ☐ Unmarried *(Single, Divorced, Widowed)*		

	Social Security No. *(SSN)*	Date of Birth *(mmddyyyy)*	Driver's License Number and State
3a Taxpayer			
3b Spouse			

Section 2: Employment Information

If the taxpayer or spouse is self-employed or has self-employment income, also complete Business Information in Sections 5 and 6.

Taxpayer		**Spouse**	
4a Taxpayer's Employer Name		5a Spouse's Employer Name	
4b Address *(Street, City, State, ZIP code)*		5b Address *(Street, City, State, ZIP code)*	
4c Work Telephone Number ( )	4d Does employer allow contact at work ☐ Yes ☐ No	5c Work Telephone Number ( )	5d Does employer allow contact at work ☐ Yes ☐ No
4e How long with this employer *(years)* *(months)*	4f Occupation	5e How long with this employer *(years)* *(months)*	5f Occupation
4g Number of exemptions claimed on Form W-4	4h Pay Period: ☐ Weekly ☐ Bi-weekly ☐ Monthly ☐ Other	5g Number of exemptions claimed on Form W-4	5h Pay Period: ☐ Weekly ☐ Bi-weekly ☐ Monthly ☐ Other

Section 3: Other Financial Information *(Attach copies of applicable documentation.)*

6 **Is the individual or sole proprietorship party to a lawsuit** *(If yes, answer the following)* Yes ☐ No ☐

☐ Plaintiff ☐ Defendant	Location of Filing	Represented by	Docket/Case No.
Amount of Suit $	Possible Completion Date *(mmddyyyy)*	Subject of Suit	

7 **Has the individual or sole proprietorship ever filed bankruptcy** *(If yes, answer the following)* Yes ☐ No ☐

Date Filed *(mmddyyyy)*	Date Dismissed or Discharged *(mmddyyyy)*	Petition No.	Location

8 **Any increase/decrease in income anticipated *(business or personal)*** *(If yes, answer the following)* Yes ☐ No ☐

Explain. *(Use attachment if needed)*	How much will it increase/decrease $	When will it increase/decrease

9 **Is the individual or sole proprietorship a beneficiary of a trust, estate, or life insurance policy** *(If yes, answer the following)* Yes ☐ No ☐

Place where recorded: EIN:

Name of the trust, estate, or policy	Anticipated amount to be received $	When will the amount be received

10 **In the past 10 years, has the individual resided outside of the United States for periods of 6 months or longer** *(If yes, answer the following)* Yes ☐ No ☐

Dates lived abroad: from *(mmddyyyy)*	To *(mmddyyyy)*

www.irs.gov Cat. No. 20312N Form **433-A** (Rev. 1-2008)

Form 433-A - Collection Information Statement for Wage Earners and Self-Employed Individuals (cont.)

Form 433-A (Rev. 1-2008) Page 2

Section 4: Personal Asset Information for All Individuals

11	**Cash on Hand.** Include cash that is not in a bank. **Total Cash on Hand**	$

Personal Bank Accounts. Include all checking, online bank accounts, money market accounts, savings accounts, stored value cards (e.g., payroll cards, government benefit cards, etc.) List safe deposit boxes including location and contents.

	Type of Account	Full Name & Address *(Street, City, State, ZIP code)* of Bank, Savings & Loan, Credit Union, or Financial Institution.	Account Number	**Account Balance** As of ______ mmddyyyy
12a				$
12b				$
12c	**Total Cash** *(Add lines 12a, 12b, and amounts from any attachments)*			$

Investments. Include stocks, bonds, mutual funds, stock options, certificates of deposit, and retirement assets such as IRAs, Keogh, and 401(k) plans. **Include all corporations, partnerships, limited liability companies or other business entities in which the individual is an officer, director, owner, member, or otherwise has a financial interest.**

	Type of Investment or Financial Interest	Full Name & Address *(Street, City, State, ZIP code)* of Company	Current Value	Loan Balance (if applicable) As of ______ mmddyyyy	**Equity** Value Minus Loan
13a		Phone	$	$	$
13b		Phone	$	$	$
13c		Phone	$	$	$
13d	**Total Equity** *(Add lines 13a through 13c and amounts from any attachments)*				$

	Available Credit. List bank issued credit cards with available credit. Full Name & Address *(Street, City, State, ZIP code)* of Credit Institution	Credit Limit	Amount Owed As of ______ mmddyyyy	**Available Credit** As of ______ mmddyyyy
14a	Acct No.:	$	$	$
14b	Acct No.:	$	$	$
14c	**Total Available Credit** *(Add lines 14a, 14b and amounts from any attachments)*			$

15a Life Insurance. Does the individual have life insurance with a cash value (Term Life insurance does not have a cash value.)
☐ **Yes** ☐ **No** If **Yes** complete blocks 15b through 15f for each policy:

15b Name and Address of Insurance Company(ies):			
15c Policy Number(s)			
15d Owner of Policy			
15e Current Cash Value	$	$	$
15f Outstanding Loan Balance	$	$	$
15g **Total Available Cash.** *(Subtract amounts on line 15f from line 15e and include amounts from any attachments)*			$

Form **433-A** (Rev. 1-2008)

Form 433-A - Collection Information Statement for Wage Earners and Self-Employed Individuals (cont.)

Form 433-A (Rev. 1-2008) Page 3

16 **In the past 10 years, have any assets been transferred by the individual for less than full value** *(If yes, answer the following. If no, skip to 17a)* Yes ☐ No ☐

List Asset	Value at Time of Transfer	Date Transferred *(mmddyyyy)*	To Whom or Where was it Transferred
	$		

Real Property Owned, Rented, and Leased. Include all real property and land contracts.

	Purchase/Lease Date *(mmddyyyy)*	Current Fair Market Value (FMV)	Current Loan Balance	Amount of Monthly Payment	Date of Final Payment *(mmddyyyy)*	**Equity** FMV Minus Loan
17a Property Description		$	$	$		$
Location *(Street, City, State, ZIP code)* and County			Lender/Lessor/Landlord Name, Address, *(Street, City, State, ZIP code)* and Phone			
17b Property Description		$	$	$		$
Location *(Street, City, State, ZIP code)* and County			Lender/Lessor/Landlord Name, Address, *(Street, City, State, ZIP code)* and Phone			

17c **Total Equity** *(Add lines 17a, 17b and amounts from any attachments)* $

Personal Vehicles Leased and Purchased. Include boats, RVs, motorcycles, trailers, etc.

Description *(Year, Mileage, Make, Model)*		Purchase/Lease Date *(mmddyyyy)*	Current Fair Market Value (FMV)	Current Loan Balance	Amount of Monthly Payment	Date of Final Payment *(mmddyyyy)*	**Equity** FMV Minus Loan
18a Year	Mileage		$	$	$		$
Make	Model	Lender/Lessor Name, Address, *(Street, City, State, ZIP code)* and Phone					
18b Year	Mileage		$	$	$		$
Make	Model	Lender/Lessor Name, Address, *(Street, City, State, ZIP code)* and Phone					

18c **Total Equity** *(Add lines 18a, 18b and amounts from any attachments)* $

Personal Assets. Include all furniture, personal effects, artwork, jewelry, collections *(coins, guns, etc.)*, antiques or other assets.

	Purchase/Lease Date *(mmddyyyy)*	Current Fair Market Value (FMV)	Current Loan Balance	Amount of Monthly Payment	Date of Final Payment *(mmddyyyy)*	**Equity** FMV Minus Loan
19a Property Description		$	$	$		$
Location *(Street, City, State, ZIP code)* and County			Lender/Lessor Name, Address, *(Street, City, State, ZIP code)* and Phone			
19b Property Description		$	$	$		$
Location *(Street, City, State, ZIP code)* and County			Lender/Lessor Name, Address, *(Street, City, State, ZIP code)* and Phone			

19c **Total Equity** *(Add lines 19a, 19b and amounts from any attachments)* $

Form **433-A** (Rev. 1-2008)

Form 433-A - Collection Information Statement for Wage Earners and Self-Employed Individuals (cont.)

Form 433-A (Rev. 1-2008) Page 4

If the taxpayer is self-employed, sections 5 and 6 must be completed before continuing.

Monthly Income/Expense Statement *(For additional information, refer to Publication 1854.)*

Total Income			Total Living Expenses			IRS USE ONLY
	Source	Gross Monthly		Expense Items [5]	Actual Monthly	Allowable Expenses
20	Wages *(Taxpayer)* [1]	$	33	Food, Clothing, and Misc. [6]	$	
21	Wages *(Spouse)* [1]	$	34	Housing and Utilities [7]	$	
22	Interest - Dividends	$	35	Vehicle Ownership Costs [8]	$	
23	Net Business Income [2]	$	36	Vehicle Operating Costs [9]	$	
24	Net Rental Income [3]	$	37	Public Transportation [10]	$	
25	Distributions [4]	$	38	Health Insurance	$	
26	Pension/Social Security *(Taxpayer)*	$	39	Out of Pocket Health Care Costs [11]	$	
27	Pension/Social Security *(Spouse)*	$	40	Court Ordered Payments	$	
28	Child Support	$	41	Child/Dependent Care	$	
29	Alimony	$	42	Life insurance	$	
30	Other (Rent subsidy, Oil credit, etc.)	$	43	Taxes *(Income and FICA)*	$	
31	Other	$	44	Other Secured Debts (Attach list)	$	
32	**Total Income** *(add lines 20-31)*	$	45	**Total Living Expenses** *(add lines 33-44)*	$	

1 **Wages, salaries, pensions, and social security:** Enter gross monthly wages and/or salaries. Do not deduct withholding or allotments taken out of pay, such as insurance payments, credit union deductions, car payments, etc. To calculate the gross monthly wages and/or salaries:
If paid weekly - multiply weekly gross wages by 4.3. Example: $425.89 x 4.3 = $1,831.33
If paid biweekly (every 2 weeks) - multiply biweekly gross wages by 2.17. Example: $972.45 x 2.17 = $2,110.22
If paid semimonthly (twice each month) - multiply semimonthly gross wages by 2. Example: $856.23 x 2 = $1,712.46

2 **Net Income from Business:** Enter monthly net business income. This is the amount earned after ordinary and necessary monthly business expenses are paid. **This figure is the amount from page 6, line 82.** If the net business income is a loss, enter "0". Do not enter a negative number. If this amount is more or less than previous years, attach an explanation.

3 **Net Rental Income:** Enter monthly net rental income. This is the amount earned after ordinary and necessary monthly rental expenses are paid. Do not include deductions for depreciation or depletion. If the net rental income is a loss, enter "0". Do not enter a negative number.

4 **Distributions:** Enter the total distributions from partnerships and subchapter S corporations reported on Schedule K-1, and from limited liability companies reported on Form 1040, Schedule C, D or E.

5 **Expenses not generally allowed:** We generally do not allow tuition for private schools, public or private college expenses, charitable contributions, voluntary retirement contributions, payments on unsecured debts such as credit card bills, cable television and other similar expenses. However, we may allow these expenses if it is proven that they are necessary for the health and welfare of the individual or family or for the production of income.

6 **Food, Clothing, and Misc.:** Total of clothing, food, housekeeping supplies, and personal care products for one month.

7 **Housing and Utilities:** For principal residence: Total of rent or mortgage payment. Add the average monthly expenses for the following: property taxes, home owner's or renter's insurance, maintenance, dues, fees, and utilities. Utilities include gas, electricity, water, fuel, oil, other fuels, trash collection, telephone, and cell phone.

8 **Vehicle Ownership Costs:** Total of monthly lease or purchase/loan payments.

9 **Vehicle Operating Costs:** Total of maintenance, repairs, insurance, fuel, registrations, licenses, inspections, parking, and tolls for one month.

10 **Public Transportation:** Total of monthly fares for mass transit (e.g., bus, train, ferry, taxi, etc.)

11 **Out of Pocket Health Care Costs:** Monthly total of medical services, prescription drugs and medical supplies (e.g., eyeglasses, hearing aids, etc.)

Certification: *Under penalties of perjury, I declare that to the best of my knowledge and belief this statement of assets, liabilities, and other information is true, correct, and complete.*

Taxpayer's Signature	Spouse's Signature	Date

Attachments Required for Wage Earners and Self-Employed Individuals:
Copies of the following items for the last 3 months from the date this form is submitted (check all attached items):

☐ Income - Earnings statements, pay stubs, etc. from each employer, pension/social security/other income, self employment income (commissions, invoices, sales records, etc.).

☐ Banks, Investments, and Life Insurance - Statements for all money market, brokerage, checking and savings accounts, certificates of deposit, IRA, stocks/bonds, and life insurance policies with a cash value.

☐ Assets - Statements from lenders on loans, monthly payments, payoffs, and balances for all personal and business assets. Include copies of UCC financing statements and accountant's depreciation schedules.

☐ Expenses - Bills or statements for monthly recurring expenses of utilities, rent, insurance, property taxes, phone and cell phone, insurance premiums, court orders requiring payments (child support, alimony, etc.), other out of pocket expenses.

☐ Other - credit card statements, profit and loss statements, all loan payoffs, etc.

☐ A copy of last year's Form 1040 with all attachments. Include all Schedules K-1 from Form 1120S or Form 1065, as applicable.

Form **433-A** (Rev. 1-2008)

Form 433-A - Collection Information Statement for Wage Earners and Self-Employed Individuals (cont.)

Form 433-A (Rev. 1-2008) Page 5

Sections 5 and 6 must be completed only if the taxpayer is SELF-EMPLOYED.

Section 5: Business Information

46 Is the business a sole proprietorship (filing Schedule C) ☐ Yes, Continue with Sections 5 and 6. ☐ No, Complete Form 433-B.
All other business entities, including limited liability companies, partnerships or corporations, must complete Form 433-B.

47 Business Name	48 Employer Identification Number	49 Type of Business Federal Contractor ☐ Yes ☐ No
50 Business Website	51 Total Number of Employees	52a Average Gross Monthly Payroll 52b Frequency of Tax Deposits

53 Does the business engage in e-Commerce (Internet sales) ☐ Yes ☐ No

	Payment Processor (e.g., PayPal, Authorize.net, Google Checkout, etc.) Name & Address (Street, City, State, ZIP code)	Payment Processor Account Number
54a		
54b		

Credit Cards Accepted by the Business.

	Credit Card	Merchant Account Number	Merchant Account Provider, Name & Address (Street, City, State, ZIP code)
55a			
55b			
55c			

56 **Business Cash on Hand.** Include cash that is not in a bank. **Total Cash on Hand** $

Business Bank Accounts. Include checking accounts, online bank accounts, money market accounts, savings accounts, and stored value cards (e.g. payroll cards, government benefit cards, etc.) *Report Personal Accounts in Section 4.*

	Type of Account	Full name & Address (Street, City, State, ZIP code) of Bank, Savings & Loan, Credit Union or Financial Institution.	Account Number	Account Balance As of ______ mmddyyyy
57a				$
57b				$

57c **Total Cash in Banks** *(Add lines 57a, 57b and amounts from any attachments)* $

Accounts/Notes Receivable. Include e-payment accounts receivable and factoring companies, and any bartering or online auction accounts. *(List all contracts separately, including contracts awarded, but not started.)* **Include Federal Government Contracts.**

	Accounts/Notes Receivable & Address (Street, City, State, ZIP code)	Status (e.g., age, factored, other)	Date Due (mmddyyyy)	Invoice Number or Federal Government Contract Number	Amount Due
58a					$
58b					$
58c					$
58d					$

58e **Total Outstanding Balance** *(Add lines 58a through 58d and amounts from any attachments)* $

Form **433-A** (Rev. 1-2008)

Form 433-A - Collection Information Statement for Wage Earners and Self-Employed Individuals (cont.)

Form 433-A (Rev. 1-2008) Page 6

Business Assets. Include all tools, books, machinery, equipment, inventory or other assets used in trade or business. Include Uniform Commercial Code *(UCC)* filings. Include Vehicles and Real Property owned/leased/rented by the business, if not shown in Section 4.

	Purchase/Lease/Rental Date *(mmddyyyy)*	Current Fair Market Value (FMV)	Current Loan Balance	Amount of Monthly Payment	Date of Final Payment *(mmddyyyy)*	**Equity** FMV Minus Loan
59a Property Description		$	$	$		$
Location *(Street, City, State, ZIP code) and County*			Lender/Lessor/Landlord Name, Address *(Street, City, State, ZIP code)* and Phone			
59b Property Description		$	$	$		$
Location *(Street, City, State, ZIP code) and County*			Lender/Lessor/Landlord Name, Address *(Street, City, State, ZIP code)* and Phone			
59c **Total Equity** *(Add lines 59a, 59b and amounts from any attachments)*						$

Section 6 should be completed only if the taxpayer is SELF-EMPLOYED

Section 6: Sole Proprietorship Information *(lines 60 through 81 should reconcile with business Profit and Loss Statement)*

Accounting Method Used: ☐ Cash ☐ Accrual

Income and Expenses during the period *(mmddyyyy)* to *(mmddyyyy)*

Total Monthly Business Income		**Total Monthly Business Expenses** *(Use attachments as needed.)*	
Source	Gross Monthly	Expense Items	Actual Monthly
60 Gross Receipts	$	70 Materials Purchased [1]	$
61 Gross Rental Income	$	71 Inventory Purchased [2]	$
62 Interest	$	72 Gross Wages & Salaries	$
63 Dividends	$	73 Rent	$
64 Cash	$	74 Supplies [3]	$
Other Income *(Specify below)*		75 Utilities/Telephone [4]	$
65	$	76 Vehicle Gasoline/Oil	$
66	$	77 Repairs & Maintenance	$
67	$	78 Insurance	$
68	$	79 Current Taxes [5]	$
		80 Other Expenses, including installment payments (Specify)	$
69 **Total Income** *(Add lines 60 through 68)*	$	81 **Total Expenses** *(Add lines 70 through 80)*	$
		82 **Net Business Income** *(Line 69 minus 81)* [6]	$

Enter the amount from line 82 on line 23, section 4. If line 82 is a loss, enter "0" on line 23, section 4.

Self-employed taxpayers must return to page 4 to sign the certification and include all applicable attachments.

1 **Materials Purchased:** Materials are items directly related to the production of a product or service.

2 **Inventory Purchased:** Goods bought for resale.

3 **Supplies:** Supplies are items used in the business that are consumed or used up within one year. This could be the cost of books, office supplies, professional equipment, etc.

4 **Utilities/Telephone:** Utilities include gas, electricity, water, oil, other fuels, trash collection, telephone and cell phone.

5 **Current Taxes:** Real estate, excise, franchise, occupational, personal property, sales and employer's portion of employment taxes.

6 **Net Business Income:** Net profit from Form 1040, Schedule C may be used if duplicated deductions are eliminated (e.g., expenses for business use of home already included in housing and utility expenses on page 4). Deductions for depreciation and depletion on Schedule C are not cash expenses and must be added back to the net income figure. In addition, interest cannot be deducted if it is already included in any other installment payments allowed.

FINANCIAL ANALYSIS OF COLLECTION POTENTIAL FOR INDIVIDUAL WAGE EARNERS AND SELF-EMPLOYED INDIVIDUALS		**(IRS USE ONLY)**
Cash Available (Lines 11, 12c, 13d, 14c, 15g, 56, 57c and 58e)	Total Cash	$
Distrainable Asset Summary (Lines 17c, 18c, 19c, and 59c)	Total Equity	$
Monthly Total Positive Income minus Expenses (Line 32 minus Line 45)	Monthly Available Cash	$

Privacy Act: The information requested on this Form is covered under Privacy Acts and Paperwork Reduction Notices which have already been provided to the taxpayer.

Form **433-A** (Rev. 1-2008)

Form 656 - Offer in Compromise

Form **656**
(February 2007)

Department of the Treasury — Internal Revenue Service

Offer in Compromise

Attach Application Fee and Payment ***(check or money order)*** **here.**

IRS RECEIVED DATE

Section I **Taxpayer Contact Information**

Taxpayer's First Name and Middle Initial	Last Name
If a joint offer, spouse's First Name and Middle Initial	Last Name
Business Name	
Taxpayer's Address *(Home or Business) (number, street, and room or suite no., city, state, ZIP code)*	
Mailing Address *(if different from above) (number, street, and room or suite no., city, state, ZIP code)*	

DATE RETURNED

Social Security Number (SSN) *(Primary)*	*(Secondary)*	Employer Identification Number (EIN) *(EIN included in offer)*	*(EIN **not** included in offer)*
- -	- -	-	-

Section II **To: Commissioner of Internal Revenue Service**

I/We *(includes all types of taxpayers)* submit this offer to compromise the tax liabilities plus any interest, penalties, additions to tax, and additional amounts required by law *(tax liability)* for the tax type and period marked below: *(Please mark an "X" in the box for the correct description and fill-in the correct tax period(s), adding additional periods if needed).*

☐ 1040/1120 Income Tax — Year(s) ____________

☐ 941 Employer's Quarterly Federal Tax Return — Quarterly period(s) ____________

☐ 940 Employer's Annual Federal Unemployment (FUTA) Tax Return — Year(s) ____________

☐ Trust Fund Recovery Penalty as a responsible person of *(enter corporation name)* ____________,

for failure to pay withholding and Federal Insurance Contributions Act taxes (Social Security taxes), for period(s) ending ____________

☐ Other Federal Tax(es) [specify type(s) and period(s)] ____________

Note: If you need more space, use a separate sheet of paper and title it "Attachment to Form 656 Dated ____________." Sign and date the attachment following the listing of the tax periods.

Section III **Reason for Offer in Compromise**

I/We submit this offer for the reason(s) checked below:

☐ Doubt as to Collectibility — "I have insufficient assets and income to pay the full amount." You must include a complete Collection Information Statement, Form 433-A and/or Form 433-B.

☐ Effective Tax Administration — "I owe this amount and have sufficient assets to pay the full amount, but due to my exceptional circumstances, requiring full payment would cause an economic hardship or would be unfair and inequitable." You must include a complete Collection Information Statement, Form 433-A and/or Form 433-B and complete Section VI.

Section IV **Offer in Compromise Terms**

I/We offer to pay $____________ *(must be more than zero)*. Complete Section VII to explain where you will obtain the funds to make this offer.

Check **only** one of the following:

☐ **Lump sum cash offer** – 20% of the amount of the offer $____________ must be sent with Form 656. Upon written acceptance of the offer, the balance must be paid in 5 or fewer installments.

$____________ payable within ________ months after acceptance
$____________ payable within ________ months after acceptance
$____________ payable within ________ months after acceptance
$____________ payable within ________ months after acceptance
$____________ payable within ________ months after acceptance

☐ **Short Term Periodic Payment Offer** – Offer amount is paid within 24 months from the date IRS received your offer. The first payment **must** be submitted with your Form 656. You **must** make regular payments during your offer investigation. Complete the following:

$____________ will be submitted with the Form 656. Beginning in the month after the offer is submitted *(insert month* ____________ *)*, on the ________ day of each month, $____________ will be sent in for a total of ________ months. *(Cannot extend more than 24 months from the date the offer was submitted.)*

Catalog Number 16728N | www.irs.gov | Form **656** (Rev. 2-2007)

Form 656 - Offer in Compromise (cont.)

Section IV Cont.

☐ **Deferred Periodic Payment Offer** – Offer amount will be paid over the remaining life of the collection statute. The first payment **must** be submitted with your Form 656. You must make regular payments during your offer investigation. Complete the following:

$ ________ will be submitted with the Form 656. Beginning in the month after the offer is submitted *(insert month* ________ *)*, on the ________ day of each month, $ ________ will be sent in for a total of ______ months.

Optional - Designation of Required Payment under IRC 7122(c)

You have the option to designate the required payment you made under Section IV above. If you chose not to designate your required payment, then the IRS will apply your payment in the best interest of the government. Please complete the following if you choose to designate your payment:

$________ paid under IRC 7122 (c) is to be applied to my ________ Tax Year/Quarter*(s) (whichever is applicable)* for my/our tax form________.

If you pay more than the required payment when you submit your offer and want any part of that additional payment treated as a deposit, check the box below and insert the amount. It is not required that you designate any portion of your payment as a deposit. **Note:** If the required payment is not paid, the offer will be returned even if you make a payment you designate as a deposit.

☐ I am making a deposit of $________ with this offer.

Section V **By submitting this offer, I/we have read, understand and agree to the following conditions:**

(a) I/We voluntarily submit all tax payments made on this offer, including the mandatory payments of tax required under section 7122(c). These tax payments are not refundable even if I/we withdraw the offer prior to acceptance or the IRS returns or rejects the offer. If the offer is accepted, the IRS will apply payments made after acceptance in the best interest of the government.

(b) Any payments made in connection with this offer will be applied to the tax liability unless I have specified that they be treated as a deposit. Only amounts that exceed the mandatory payments can be treated as a deposit. Such a deposit will be refundable if the offer is rejected or returned by the IRS or is withdrawn. I/we understand that the IRS will not pay interest on any deposit.

(c) The application fee for this offer will be kept by the IRS unless the offer was not accepted for processing.

(d) I/We will comply with all provisions of the Internal Revenue Code relating to filing my/our returns and paying my/our required taxes for 5 years or until the offered amount is paid in full, whichever is longer. In the case of a jointly submitted Offer in Compromise joint liabilities, I/we understand that default with respect to the compliance provisions described in this paragraph by one party to this agreement will not result in the default of the entire agreement. The default provisions described in Section V(i) of this agreement will be applied only to the party failing to comply with the requirements of this paragraph.

(e) I/We waive and agree to the suspension of any statutory periods of limitation (time limits provided by law) for the IRS assessment of the liability for the periods identified in Section II. I/We understand that I/we have the right not to waive these statutory periods or to limit the waiver to a certain length or to certain periods. I/We understand, however, that the IRS may not consider this offer if I/we refuse to waive the statutory periods for assessment or if we provide only a limited waiver. The amount of any Federal tax due for the periods described in Section II may be assessed at any time prior to the acceptance of this offer or within one year of the rejection of this offer. I/We understand that the statute of limitations for collection will be suspended during the period an offer is considered pending by the IRS (paragraph (k) of this section defines pending).

(f) The IRS will keep all payments and credits made, received or applied to the total original liability before submission of this offer and all payments required under section 7122(c). The IRS will also keep all payments in excess of those required by section 7122(c) that are received in connection with the offer and that are not designated as deposits in Section IV. The IRS may keep any proceeds from a levy served prior to submission of the offer, but not received at the time the offer is submitted. As additional consideration beyond the amount of my/our offer, the IRS will keep any refund, including interest, due to me/us because of overpayment of any tax or other liability, for tax periods extending through the calendar year in which the IRS accepts the offer. The date of acceptance is the date on the written notice of acceptance issued by the IRS to me/us or to my/our representative. I/We may not designate an overpayment ordinarily subject to refund, to which the IRS is entitled, to be applied to estimated tax payments for the following year.

(g) I/We will return to the IRS any refund identified in paragraph (f) received after submission of this offer.

(h) The IRS cannot collect more than the full amount of the liability under this offer.

(i) I/We understand that I/we remain responsible for the full amount of the liabilities, unless and until the IRS accepts the offer in writing and I/we have met all the terms and conditions of the offer. The IRS will not remove the original amount of the liabilities from its records until I/we have met all the terms and conditions of the offer. I/We understand that the liabilities I/we offer to compromise are and will remain liabilities until I/we meet all the terms and conditions of this offer. If I/we file for bankruptcy before the terms and conditions of this offer are completed, any claim the IRS files in the bankruptcy proceedings will be a tax claim.

(j) Once the IRS accepts the offer in writing, I/we have no right to contest, in court or otherwise, the amount of the liability.

(k) The offer is pending starting with the date an authorized IRS official signs the form. The offer remains pending until an authorized IRS official accepts, rejects, returns or acknowledges withdrawal of the offer in writing. If I/we appeal an IRS rejection decision on the offer, IRS will continue to treat the offer as pending until the Appeals Office accepts or rejects the offer in writing.

Form 656 - Offer in Compromise (cont.)

If I/we don't file a protest within 30 days of the date the IRS notifies me/us of the right to protest the decision, I/we waive the right to a hearing before the Appeals Office about the Offer in Compromise.

(l) If I/we fail to meet any of the terms and conditions of the offer and the offer defaults, the IRS may:

- immediately file suit to collect the entire unpaid balance of the offer;
- immediately file suit to collect an amount equal to the original amount of the liability, minus any payment already received under the terms of this offer;
- disregard the amount of the offer and apply all amounts already paid under the offer against the original amount of the liability; and/or
- file suit or levy to collect the original amount of the liability, without further notice of any kind.

The IRS will continue to add interest, as section 6601 of the Internal Revenue Code requires, on the amount the IRS determines is due after default. The IRS will add interest from the date the offer is defaulted until I/we completely satisfy the amount owed.

(m) The IRS generally files a Notice of Federal Tax Lien to protect the Government's interest on offers with deferred payments. Also, the IRS may file a Notice of Federal Tax Lien during the offer investigation. This tax lien will be released when the payment terms of the offer agreement have been satisfied.

(n) I/We understand that IRS employees may contact third parties in order to respond to this request and I/we authorize the IRS to make such contacts. Further, by authorizing the IRS to contact third parties, I/we understand that I/we will not receive notice, pursuant to section 7602(c) of the Internal Revenue Code, of third parties contacted in connection with this request.

(o) I/We are offering to compromise all the liabilities assessed against me/us as of the date of this offer and under the taxpayer identification numbers listed in Section II above. I/We authorize the IRS to amend Section II, above, to include any assessed liabilities we failed to list on Form 656.

Section VI Explanation of Circumstances

I am requesting an Offer in Compromise for the reason(s) listed below:

Note: *If you believe you have special circumstances affecting your ability to fully pay the amount due, explain your situation. You may attach additional sheets if necessary. Please include your name and SSN or EIN on all additional sheets or supporting documentation.*

Section VII Source of Funds

I / We shall obtain the funds to make this offer from the following source(s):

Catalog Number 16728N www.irs.gov Form **656** (Rev. 2-2007)

Form 656 - Offer in Compromise (cont.)

Page 4 of 4

Section VIII **Mandatory Signatures**

Taxpayer Attestation

If I / We submit this offer on a substitute form, I/ we affirm that this form is a verbatim duplicate of the official Form 656, and I/we agree to be bound by all the terms and conditions set forth in the official Form 656.

Under penalties of perjury, I declare that I have examined this offer, including accompanying schedules and statements, and to the best of my knowledge and belief, it is true, correct and complete.

Signature of Taxpayer	Date
Signature of Taxpayer	Date

Official Use Only

I accept the waiver of the statutory period of limitations on assessment for the Internal Revenue Service, as described in Section V(e).

Signature of Authorized Internal Revenue Service Official	Title	Date

Section IX **Application Prepared by Someone Other than the Taxpayer**

If this application was prepared by someone other than the taxpayer, please fill in that person's name and address below.

Name

Address *(if known) (Street, City, State, ZIP code)*

Section X **Paid Preparer Use Only**

Name of Preparer

Signature of Preparer	Date	Check if self-employed ☐	Preparer's CAF no. or PTIN

Firm's name (or yours if self-employed), address, and ZIP code	EIN
	Telephone number ( )

Section XI **Third Party Designee**

Do you want to allow another person to discuss this offer with the IRS? ☐ Yes. Complete the information below. ☐ No

Designee's name	Telephone number ( )

Privacy Act Statement

We ask for the information on this form to carry out the internal revenue laws of the United States. Our authority to request this information is Section 7801 of the Internal Revenue Code.

Our purpose for requesting the information is to determine if it is in the best interests of the IRS to accept an Offer in Compromise. You are not required to make an Offer in Compromise; however, if you choose to do so, you must provide all of the taxpayer information requested. Failure to provide all of the information may prevent us from processing your request.

If you are a paid preparer and you prepared the Form 656 for the taxpayer submitting an offer, we request that you complete and sign Section X on Form 656, and provide identifying information. Providing this information is voluntary. This information will be used to administer and enforce the internal revenue laws of the United States and may be used to regulate practice before the Internal Revenue Service for those persons subject to Treasury Department Circular No. 230, Regulations Governing the Practice of Attorneys, Certified Public Accountants, Enrolled Agents, Enrolled Actuaries, and Appraisers before the Internal Revenue Service. Information on this form may be disclosed to the Department of Justice for civil and criminal litigation.

We may also disclose this information to cities, states and the District of Columbia for use in administering their tax laws and to combat terrorism. Providing false or fraudulent information on this form may subject you to criminal prosecution and penalties.

Catalog Number 16728N www.irs.gov Form **656** (Rev. 2-2007)

Final Thoughts

I trust you found the information in this book helpful.

My goal in sharing it with you is to give you the basic information needed to solve your IRS tax problem.

I hope you now better understand the ways the IRS works, and that there *is* a solution to your problem.

But you must take the first step.

I know that moving forward into an unknown process like dealing with the IRS is scary, and not something that you look forward to doing.

But I promise you, after you take the first steps to begin to solve your problem, there will be a lifting of anxiety, and you will be well on the way to getting the IRS out of your life.

About the Author

Larry M. Weinstein is a CPA (Texas) and Certified Tax Resolution Specialist from Houston, Texas.

He is the Managing Director of SolveMyTaxProblems.com.

Larry graduated from the University of Houston with a BBA in Accounting and began his career in the Houston office of Arthur Young (now known as Ernst & Young).

In private practice since 1988, Larry concentrates his practice in the area of IRS Problem Resolution as well as in tax preparation and planning.

Having worked with hundreds of individuals and families around the country who have had some type of problem with the IRS, Larry's assistance in solving their problems with the IRS have helped his clients get their lives back on track.

Larry is the developer of the **Strategic IRS Tax Problem Resolution Process™.**

Larry lives in Houston with his wife and two daughters. When he is not watching his girls compete in lacrosse and cheerleading, he enjoys photography, fishing, and riding his motor scooter.

Made in United States
North Haven, CT
04 November 2026

21763949R00055